PRAISE FOR
Tradition and the Black Atlantic

"Mapping the contested concept of culture in diasporic, post-colonial and multicultural spaces, Henry Louis Gates, Jr. conveys far-reaching insights in a piquant style that never fails to stimulate and provoke. What results is a critical cosmopolitanism that puts him at the heart of humanist inquiry in an era of global change."

—Kobena Mercer, author of *Welcome to the Jungle*

"Anyone who imagines 'the Black community' as a place of un-questioning solidarity or groupthink will be awakened from their slumber by Gates's brilliant exploration of the fault lines in Black discourse and race-thinking. Who remembers that Richard Wright thought the European conquest of Africa was a good thing? Who knew how much Marxist cultural studies owes to arch-conservative Edmund Burke? Who imagined that Patrick Buchanan might be right in characterizing the 'culture wars' as a battle for the soul of America? This lively and learned book should be required reading for anyone who wants to understand the American soul in a glob-alizing world."

—W. J. T. Mitchell, Professor of English and Art History at the University of Chicago, and editor of *Critical Theory*

TRADITION
and the
BLACK ATLANTIC

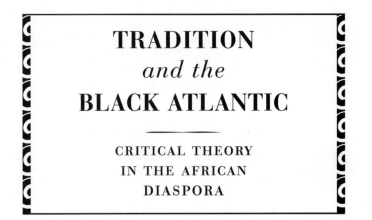

TRADITION
and the
BLACK ATLANTIC

CRITICAL THEORY
IN THE AFRICAN
DIASPORA

Henry Louis Gates, Jr.

BASIC
CIVITAS
BOOKS

A Member of the Perseus Books Group
New York

Excerpts of chapters in this book have appeared in *Critical Inquiry* 17, no. 3 and 34, no. 2, in *Black American Cinema*, ed. Manthia Diawara (London: Routledge, 1993), and in *Profession 93*.

Books published by BasicCivitas are available at special discounts for bulk purchases in the United States by corporations, institutions, and other organizations. For more information, please contact the Special Markets Department at the Perseus Books Group, 2300 Chestnut Street, Suite 200, Philadelphia, PA 19103, or call (800) 810-4145, ext. 5000, or e-mail special.markets@perseusbooks.com.

Designed by Pauline Brown
Typeset in 13 point Arno Pro

Library of Congress Cataloging-in-Publication Data

Gates, Henry Louis.
    Tradition and the Black Atlantic : critical theory in the African diaspora / Henry Louis Gates, Jr.
        p.   cm.
    Includes bibliographical references and index.
    ISBN 978-0-465-01410-1 (alk. paper)
    1.   African Americans—Race identity.   2.   Blacks—Race identity—Great Britain.   3.   Multiculturalism—Philosophy.   4. Multiculturalism—United States.   5. Multiculturalism—Great Britain.   6. Culture conflict—United States.   7. Critical theory. I. Title.
    E185.61.G254 2010
    305.896'073—dc22

                                                              2010013437

10 9 8 7 6 5 4 3 2 1

For Stuart Hall

"Black" does not reference a particular group, with fixed characteristics, whose social being or artistic imagination is determined by skin colour, genetic make-up or biological inheritance. It does not invoke an essentialized cultural identity, frozen in time, which is automatically transmitted into the work, and can thus be held to "represent" collectively all those who belong to a particular "race," ethnic community, or tradition. "Black," as deployed here, is a politically, historically and culturally constructed category; a contested idea, whose ultimate destination remains unsettled.

STUART HALL AND MARK SEALY, *DIFFERENT: A HISTORICAL CONTEXT, CONTEMPORARY PHOTOGRAPHERS, AND BLACK IDENTITY*

Contents

Preface

> *A damaging system of representation can
> only be dismantled, not by a sudden dose
> of "the real," but by another, alternative
> system of representation, whose form bet-
> ter approximates the complexity of the real
> relations it seeks to explore and contest.*
>
> STUART HALL, "ASSEMBLING THE 1980s:
> THE DELUGE—AND AFTER"

My interest in the ways that writers and thinkers in the Anglo-African literary tradition of the eighteenth century (which Robert Farris Thompson defined as "the Trans-Atlantic" tradition and which Paul Gilroy has memorably named the "Black Atlantic" tradition) formally influenced and self-consciously read and revised each other's texts had its beginnings in my graduate work under Wole Soyinka and Charles T. Davis in the faculties of English at the University of Cambridge and at Yale between 1973 and 1978.

That work culminated in a doctoral thesis exploring the role of writing in the larger discourse of race and reason during the Enlightenment and more specifically the critical reception of black writers in England and America between 1750 and 1830. A vastly revised version of that thesis will be published as *Black Letters and the Enlightenment.*

The four chapters of this book in their original form were written between 1989 and 1992 in an attempt to organize my thinking about the British Black Arts Movement of the 1980s and the American "culture wars," which were raging within and about the academy at roughly the same time, especially following the Republican National Convention in 1992. However, the Black Arts Movement in Britain and the culture wars in the United States continued to evolve during the 1990s, so I continued to revise and expand my thinking about both. I seized opportunities to share my thinking about both phenomena to various academic audiences—initially as the Richard Wright Lectures in 1989 at the University of Pennsylvania's Center for the Study of Black Literature and Culture, and three years later, in a much fuller version, as the Clarendon Lectures at the University of Oxford, and in dozens of lectures throughout the 1990s— taking into account further developments in both.

And what has been the fate of these two cultural movements? The Black Arts Movement in Britain— pronounced to be "over" by some of its key participants as early as 1990 and all but dead by the end of the century—remains, in various novel guises, a live and vibrant cultural force in Britain and has become institutionalized in the American academy through the "cultural studies" criticism of writers such as Stuart Hall, Paul Gilroy, Hazel V. Carby, and Kobena Mercer, among others, and in the art world through the work of its major visual artists in various media, especially in film, video, photography, and painting. Unfortunately, the culture wars have not diminished in ferocity in this country since the early 1990s debates about the literary canon, and they seem destined to rage on—in forms we could scarcely imagine back then—such as Tea Party debates over the policies of our nation's first black president. Barack Obama's occupancy in the White House has profoundly redefined the forms that a "culture war" can assume. As Charles M. Blow put it recently, "The Apostles of Anger in their echo chamber of fallacies have branded him the enemy. This has now become an article of faith. Obama isn't just the enemy of small government and national solvency. He is the enemy of liberty."[1]

Despite the extensive revisions that I have done since delivering those two lecture series, this book retains the intention and spirit of the original lectures. It is, I hope, a modest attempt at beginning to understand the unfolding of two very important cultural movements, one abroad, one at home; some of their key themes and trends; and the implications of both movements on the culture that we create and analyze and in which we live today here in the United States and in Britian.

A full historical account and critical overview of the British Black Arts Movement would be outside of the purview of *Tradition and the Black Atlantic*, but as we shall see, this radical cultural movement achieved an important and—in the history of black cultural movements—a unique form of institutionalization (at least of a key part of that extraordinary movement) during its third decade in the form of the founding of Rivington Place. This magnificent visual arts center, designed by Ghanaian architect David Adjaye, has been the home since 2007 of Autograph ABP (Association of Black Photographers) and Iniva, the International Institute of Visual Arts, a project funded by a £5.9 million grant from the Arts Council of England Lottery Capital 2 grant and a £1.1 million grant from Barclays Bank. Rivington Place is also the home of the Stuart Hall Library, and it is to Stuart Hall that this book is dedicated.

—HENRY LOUIS GATES, JR.,
CAMBRIDGE, MASSACHUSETTS, APRIL 15, 2010

Chapter One

Enlightenment's Esau

Prologue: The Wright Stuff?

Before Richard Wright sat the third world of theory.

It was Friday evening, September 21, 1956. The occasion was the First International Conference of Negro Writers and Artists, held at the Sorbonne's Amphithéâtre Descartes in Paris, now in its third day.

In the audience sat, expectantly, Alioune Diop of Senegal—"tall, very dark, and self-contained," James Baldwin put it, "and who rather resembles, in his extreme sobriety, an old-time Baptist minister"—the editor of *Présence Africaine*, the principal organizer of the conference, and the man whom Léopold Senghor would memorialize as "the Black Socrates"; poet Aimé Césaire of Martinique; physicist and historian Cheikh-Anta Diop of Senegal; psychiatrist and political philosopher Dr. Frantz Fanon of Martinique and Algeria; novelist George Lamming of Barbados; Dr. Jean Price-Mars, at eighty the elder statesman of the group and the president of the conference, whom James Baldwin described as "a very old and very handsome man"; novelist Jacques Stephen Alexis, like Price-Mars from Haiti; Léopold Sédar Senghor, Césaire's fellow student at the Lycée Louis-le-Grand, where they had met and founded the Négritude Movement in 1935, and who almost exactly four years from this evening would be elected the first president of the Republic of Senegal— just to begin a long and glorious roll call. With the conspicuous exception of Dr. W. E. B. Du Bois, now eighty-eight, who had been denied a passport by the U.S. State Department—"I am not present at your meeting," Du Bois's message to the gathering began, "because the U.S. government will not give me a passport," adding for good measure a jibe at the Americans sitting in the amphitheatre: "Any American Negro traveling abroad today must either not care about Negroes or say what the State Department wishes him to say"[1]— here was assembled practically every major black critical thinker of the age. Here, gathered in the Amphithéâtre Descartes, itself one of the West's most sacred and lavishly conspicuous icons of and tributes to the triumph of Reason and the spirit of Enlightenment over the dark worlds of superstition and pagan beliefs, sat the authors of third world liberation, world-historic theorists of colonial resistance, forging new ideologies, new analyses, new "weapons of theory" out of Négritude, Marxism, psychoanalysis, African communalism, you name it. Remember, it was 1956 and these were the heady days of grand theory for the black world. Never had the promise of a genuine politics of culture seemed more real, more realizable.

And before them stood Richard Wright. Two years shy of his fiftieth birthday, he was bespectacled, wearing a three-piece suit and a white shirt, his hair close-cropped. The photograph's a little fuzzy, but it's easy to make out the familiar visages of post-colonial iconography. His presence, and his lecture, had been eagerly awaited. After all, Richard Wright was, in 1956, easily the most famous, and most successful, black novelist in the world.

Nor was Wright completely insensible of the burden upon him: "So great a legion of ideological interests is choking the atmosphere of the world today," he declared, "that I deem it wise to define the terms in which I speak and for whom. All public utterances these days are branded for and against something or somebody."[2]

The remarks that followed made his own allegiances quite clear, and you have to admire his courage. For Wright's chief argument was that colonialism was the best thing that had ever befallen the continent of Africa. However venal the motivation of the European colonizers, he was emphatic that they "could not have done a better job of liberating the masses of Asia and Africa from their age-old traditions." As he continued, "Today, a knowing black, brown, or yellow man can say: 'Thank you, Mr. White Man, for freeing me from the rot of my irrational traditions and customs.'"[3]

Wright had an acute sense of what Gayatri Spivak has dubbed the "epistemic violence" of colonialism, and he applauded it. It made him giddy with a delicious sense of possibility. "In the minds of hundreds of millions of Asians and Africans," he asserted, "the traditions of their lives have been psychologically condemned beyond recall." Moreover, he continued, "millions live uneasily with beliefs of which they have been made ashamed. I say, '*Bravo!*' . . . Not to the motives, mind you. . . . But I do say, '*Bravo!*' to the consequences of Western plundering, a plundering that created the conditions for the possible rise of rational societies for the greater majority of mankind.[4]"

It gets better. As Wright explained:

> The spirit of the Enlightenment, of the Reformation which made Europe great now has a chance to be extended to all mankind! A part of the non-West is now akin to a part of the West. . . . The partial overcoming of the forces of tradition and oppressive religions in Europe resulted, in a round-about manner, in a partial overcoming of tradition and religion in decisive parts of Asia and Africa. The unspoken assumption in this history has been: WHAT IS GOOD FOR EUROPE IS GOOD FOR ALL MANKIND! I say: So be it.
>
> I agree with what has happened.

Wright regretted not what Europe did, but only that it "could . . . have done what [it] did in a deliberate and intentional manner, could have planned it as a global project," one performed out of a "sense of lofty responsibility."[5]

Talk about lucking out. Happy campers of the third world, Africa, you see, had won the Publishers Clearing House sweepstakes of history—the jackpot

of Enlightenment rationalism—and was too be-
nighted to appreciate it.

There's more. In Wright's eyes, the Western-
educated elite in Africa "constitutes islands of free
men, the FREEST MEN IN ALL THE WORLD
TODAY," those last seven words printed in all caps.
And the task of the West was now to help this cadre
of free men in every way to complete the epistemic
violence of colonialism and, as he put it, "establish
rational areas of living."[6]

And because these were the freest men in the
world today, it was crucial that they be given their
head to use, as Wright recommended, *"dictatorial
means"* (my italics) to set their houses in order. "Let
the Africans and Asians whom you have educated in
Europe have their freedom," he said. And the particular freedom he had in mind was—as he was at pains
to make clear—the freedom to oppress their own
people. How else could they be liberated from the
stultifying burden of those superstitions and traditions that had survived colonialism? He concluded
with a ringing declaration: "Freedom is indivisible."[7]

Irony was, of course, not Richard Wright's strong
suit. But I don't know if this was ever more painfully
displayed than in the words he chose to conclude
what was, after all, a blueprint for a neocolonialist po-

lice state. Still, we can at least credit him with a fair degree of historical prescience.

Now the story I have been telling is scarcely unknown in African American letters, at least in outline. James Baldwin, in summary fashion, gave an eloquent account in *Encounter* magazine of his own reactions to the conference. Most memorably, Baldwin noted, with mordant irony, Wright's statement that "what was good for Europe was good for all mankind" was "a tactless way of phrasing a debatable idea." Baldwin then went on to say that the idea that these brown and black dictators would voluntarily surrender their "personal power" (Wright's phrase) "once the new social order had been established" was pure fantasy: "I suppose it would be the second coming."[8] (Senghor, however, bucking a vile trend, would eventually surprise the Continent and do just that.)

And if I may make the sort of confession that, perhaps, a critic should never make, my reading at the age of fifteen of Baldwin's fascinating account of the conference in *Notes of a Native Son* is one reason that I've always borne a certain ambivalence about the writings of Richard Wright. The other reason is Wright's own deep ambivalence toward traditional African culture and to the place of Africans in what we might call the "great black chain of being," as he made clear in 1954 in his book *Black Power*, about Ghana's coming independence, ominously subtitled *A Record of Reactions in a Land of Pathos*. Wright made it clear in this book that he was no champion of Pan-Africanism or black cultural nationalism. And frankly, precisely because of these attitudes expressed in *Black Power* and at the 1956 Paris conference, I've never understood how Wright, of all people, could have become one of the patron saints of the Black Arts Movement in America in the 1960s, a movement not best recalled for its close readings of the black canon.

In fact, I believe that the celebration of Wright by black arts critics such as Addison Gayle as the summit of radical black nationalism in the African American canon had everything to do with the fact that Bigger Thomas, the protagonist of Wright's best-selling *Native Son*, accidentally murders the daughter of his wealthy white employer and then intentionally beheads her and stuffs her body parts into a furnace. But no credible reader, in the 1960s or now, could possibly hold up Richard Wright as a model for Pan-Africanism. Indeed, Wright and his former friend, rival, and eventual literary antagonist, Ralph Ellison, curiously enough, shared this seeming aversion to Africa and its Africans. They saw the American Negro, just as Kenneth Clarke and the early Melville Herskovits did, as sui generis, the Middle Passage as an event so traumatic as to make the people who emerged from the nightmare of the slave ships a new kind of black person, a tabula rasa, Africa erased from their culture, their traditions, their language, their belief systems, their consciousnesses, like chalk erases words and symbols on a chalkboard.[9] I have to believe that at least some of the members of his audience on that evening in September 1956 could not help thinking: "Thank you, Mister Wright man, for freeing me from the rot of my irrational traditions. Maybe someday I'll return the favor."

There's a further irony that I think has never really been brought out. Wright was delivering a paper he'd composed beforehand, and he was delivering it after most of the other participants in the conference had made their pronouncements. And as you might expect, he had some doubts about whether he should modify his paper in light of what he'd heard. But not for the reason you might expect, not because he was in the least impressed by the sophistication of his fellow speakers, many of whom we would identify as germinal theorists of national liberation. On the contrary, incredibly, by the end of the day he found himself persuaded that these primitive Africans were so backward, so unenlightened, so unevolved, that he doubted that they would even be able to *take in* the subtleties of his analysis.

It is intriguing to compare the version of Wright's paper, called "Tradition and Industrialization," as it appears in his collection *White Man, Listen,* to the relatively verbatim version published as part of the conference proceedings in *Présence Africaine* and from which I have been quoting. Whereas in the paper that he wrote beforehand, he joyously looked forward to the secularization of Africa, at the conference he registered his considerable disappointment. He interjected remarks such as, "When I wrote that statement, I was hoping and dreaming for black freedom. But after listening to the gentleman of the cloth who spoke here this morning . . . I wonder now if I can say that Africa is more secular-minded than the West." And later on, he broke off from his exaltation of Africa's Westernized elites to observe, "Again, I must check and correct my perceptions against the reality, mainly religious in nature, that has emerged from this conference."[10] But he'd already expressed his disappointment in the conference at a roundtable the day before: "I thought that with the political situation shaping up rapidly, we could have addressed ourselves in a concrete manner about why [African] culture was so easily shattered and how we could have gone about . . . modifying what seemed to be perhaps its too deeply subjective content; draining it off into objectivities and instrumentalities, that would have enabled a section of the ground to be cleared for the erection of concrete projects." These, he told us, were "the 'live' questions from which we could have started grappling from the first day."[11] (And it is important that we remember, too, this vision of a base culture transmuted into golden "objectivities and instrumentalities.")[12]

So Wright had a strong conviction of being in a backwater, betrayed by the theoretical equivalent of what Marxist theory used to call "uneven development." And in a funny way, his sense of being "out of time," temporally disjointed with the third world participants, was somehow echoed in the fact that every time Wright spoke, he glanced at his watch. This runs through the record of the proceedings like a leitmotif. Wright's formal presentation opened with the words "The hour is late, and I am pressed for time." The day before, as a participant in a roundtable, he began with the words "Ladies and Gentlemen, I shall be as brief as possible: the hour is late."[13] He was the White Rabbit in *Alice in Wonderland*.

And I note this tiny detail not to labor Wright's remarkable, one might say colonial, condescension toward his third world compeers, for I think perhaps the hour was late, historically speaking, too late for Richard Wright. His vision of Africa didn't seem much of an advance on that of, say, nineteenth-century Pan-Africanist Edward Wilmot Blyden. For Wright, Africa was still a place, as Blyden had put it, "in a state of barbarism." (Here, Wright and his former friend, Ralph Ellison, would have been in hearty agreement. Baldwin's attitudes toward Africa were also complex. Of the "big three" authors in the mid-century African American literary canon, only Wright would actually set foot in sub-Saharan Africa.) On the evening of the first day, just two days before, in a wide-ranging discussion on the nature of culture, Senghor had enthusiastically and generously extended to Wright the warmest and most encompassing embrace that his Afro-cosmopolitanism could muster, declaring that a poem of Wright's and especially his autobiography, *Black Boy*, were in form and function, aesthetically and subconsciously, irresistibly and inevitably "African." They were fundamental parts or extensions of a Pan-African canon, a collective "African autobiography," as a startled Baldwin would write, "like one more book in the Bible, speaking of the African's long persecution and exile."[14] Perhaps only through the glasses of one of the fathers of Négritude could one see the subtle degree of intertextuality between, say, *The Palm Wine Drinkard* and Wright's autobiographical rendition of the trope of the noble savage.

Two days later, Wright would make it clear that he had recoiled at the embrace. And maybe it's worth insisting on the fact that Wright's use of the Western category of "religion" concealed a larger freight: What does the word signify in nonsecular, nonindustrial, non-Western societies where, as Wright knew and lamented, no inpenetrable partition exists between religious practices and everyday life? In this sort of context, the word "religion" can be used only as a surrogate for "culture." What Africa needed finally to shed, in Wright's view, was nothing less than traditional African culture itself. Unable to conceive of any counter-hegemonic possibilities in autochthonous cultures, then, Wright could see, in the work of these third world intellectuals, only the dismal prospect of an Africa that would not cease to be African.

———

But my target here is actually not Richard Wright at all. If, as Wright would have it, there's a Bigger Thomas in all of us American Negroes, I want to argue that there's a Richard Wright in our generation of diasporic intellectuals. In the sense that we are Wright's heirs, I want to test that line from Ezekiel: "The fathers have eaten sour grapes, and the children's teeth are set on edge." Because it won't do just to say that Wright made some funny choices, and if my exposition sets anybody's teeth on edge, I want to explore why.

Wright's stature as a black intellectual is beyond question. As Paul Gilroy has perceptively noted, he was "one of a handful of black writers who have seen black nationalism as a beginning rather than an end."[15] (In Chapter 2, I try to explore some of the paradoxes around this issue.) But there's a fissure, a fault line—sometimes it can be a hairline fracture, sometimes a real break—that runs through Wright and through us when we're trying to talk about cultural imperialism. It doesn't start with Wright, though. I want to trace it further back. And this is where things start to get a little weird, because Wright himself told us where to start looking.

When Wright said that Europe's great gift to the third world was the Enlightenment, he very explicitly located it as the historic, capital-E Enlightenment, the flowering of European rationalism and universalism, what Will and Ariel Durant would call the Age of Reason. It was also the age in which mercantile networks were consolidated into the modern colonial state. I want to follow Richard Wright's lead here.

Enlightenment's Esau

So I'm going to summon a rather prophetic eighteenth-century figure who not only anticipated the post-colonialist critique of Enlightenment rationalism, but who also may have founded the discourse against imperialism with which we align ourselves today. His was in so many ways the perfect ideological antagonist to Wright's position. But more than that, he was, and perhaps remains, the most powerful critic of the modern colonial state, which he tried to strangle in its crib. The anti-imperialist credo has had no more powerful rhetorician. His campaign against the British administration in India, then in corporate/parastatal form, preoccupied him for two decades. Moreover, his was a critique that apprehended fully the violence, both material and cultural, that the political economy of colonialism inflicted upon subject peoples. Nothing was more abhorrent to him than the coercive eradication of India's diverse, indigenous traditions.

Here was a man who, almost single-handedly, took on the most powerful instrumentality of empire, the man who led an eight-year-long prosecution of one Warren Hastings, governor of Bengal, head of the East India Trading Company. Toward the end of his life, this man wrote, "Let everything I have done, said, or written be forgotten but this."[16] And yet he never really expected his impeachment to succeed. What mattered to him was enacting a theater, a public spectacle, that would expose the human cruelties of the colonial regime. So his impossible task was, in the first instance, a dramatic, rather than a legal, endeavor, as he argued, as early as 1783. "We are on a conspicuous stage, and the world marks our demeanor."[17] The trial was yet to begin, but the prosecutor had, by this point, been studying the matter of India for eighteen years.

The indictment of Warren Hastings was more than a study of personification, more than impeachment by synecdoche, but it was that, too. As our prosecutor wrote, "It is not the culprit who is upon its trial, it is the House of Lords that is upon its trial, it is the British nation that is upon its trial before all other nations, before the present generation, and before a long, long posterity."[18]

In almost Fanonian cadences, he detailed the crippling physical tortures visited on the hapless natives and ventured that a day of reckoning could not long be deferred: The time will arrive, he warned, when "crippled and disabled hands will act with resistless power. What is it that they will not pull down, when they are lifted to heaven against their oppressors? Then, what can withstand such hands? Can the powers that crushed and destroyed them?" "We may bite our chains if will, but we shall be made to know ourselves."[19]

The figure I summon, the father of anti-colonialism, is, of course Edmund Burke—probably not a paternity most of us would freely choose, at least not at first glance. It makes life easier when our radicals aren't also reactionaries, when our anti-imperialists don't partake of the imperial vision as well. Easier, but also less instructive.

But let's first grant him the historical prescience we granted Wright. "It is," Burke admonished,

the nature of tyranny and rapacity never to learn moderation from the ill-success of first oppressions; on the contrary, all oppressors, all men thinking highly of the methods dictated by their nature, attribute the frustration of their desire to the want of sufficient rigor. Then they redouble the efforts of their impotent cruelty, which, producing, as they ever must produce, new disappointments, they grow irritated against the objects of their rapacity; and then rage, fury, malice, implacable because unprovoked, recruiting and reinforcing their avarice, their vices are no longer human.

And in these words, he mapped out the course of colonialism in the century and a half to come. So when Burke claimed, about his prosecution of Warren Hastings, that his concern was "not only to state the fact, but to assign the criminality; to fix the *species* of that criminality," I want to suggest that he fixed it—something we'd call colonial guilt—for posterity as well.[20]

And to bolster my case, I want quickly to sketch three elements of the Burkean critique of imperialism. (And it has to be done, because historically speaking there are at least four barriers that any rereading of Burke has to handle. In reverse chronological order, these are, first, the misappropriation of Burke as a natural law proponent in the 1950s, which reinforced his popular appropriation as the "father of modern conservatism"—the sort of cartoon anti-Communist still touted by Irving Kristol and George Will and others. Second, and ironically, there's the Victorian celebration of Burke as a kind of Benthamite liberal, of all things. Third, there are, of course, the Jacobin critiques of his contemporaries—Thomas Paine and

William Godwin and so on. And fourth, there are influential nineteenth-century misreadings produced by people such as Thomas Macaulay. So there's this whole obstacle course in the history of ideas that's already set up for us.)[21]

Now, the first element—which I want to pass over quickly, because it's least relevant to my argument— is that Burke was the first to propose a theory of colonial extraction, known as the "drainage" theory, that was to become an extremely important subject in later Indian historiography. It's worth noting that almost half of Burke's published work concerns India in one way or another, and this particular stuff isn't in the trial proceedings. It's in his *Ninth Report* on the East India Trading Company's government, where he wrote about the "ruin of Bengal's traditional economy," the decline of native handicrafts, and the corporate techniques used to accomplish both. But his boldest observation was that, as he wrote, "the whole exported produce of the country (so far as the Company is concerned) is not exchanged in the course of barter; but is taken away without any return or payment whatsoever. . . . The country has suffered, what is tantamount to an annual plunder of its manufactures and its produce to the value of twelve hundred thousand pounds." Indeed, "the whole foreign maritime trade, whether English, French, Dutch, or Danish, arises from the revenues: and these are carried out of the country, without producing any thing to compensate so heavy a loss."[22]

The interesting thing is that, even while Karl Marx was deriding Burke as "an out and out vulgar bourgeois" (not to mention a "celebrated sophist and sycophant"),[23] he borrowed Burke's "drainage" theory whole cloth, which is, if I may say so, another form of unrequited import: the transfer of ideas from Burke to Marx. Maybe it's worth noting that if you take the concept of cultural imperialism seriously, the pair makes for an ironic contrast. Let's take an example. In an article written for the *New York Tribune* of June 25, 1853, Karl Marx satirized the villages in Hindustan, charging that "they subjected man to external circumstances instead of elevating man to the sovereign of circumstances. . . . They transformed a self-developing social state into never changing natural destiny, and thus brought about a brutalizing worship of nature, exhibiting its degradation in the fact that man, the sovereign of nature, fell down on his knees in adoration of Hanuman, the monkey, and Sabbala, the cow."[24] In contrast, Burke argued strenuously for the beauty and integrity of these customs, these forms of alterity, however alien to an Englishman.

Even when Richard Wright became a fierce anti-Communist in the 1940s and 1950s, he remained absolutely faithful to Marx in at least this one respect. Marx lauded Britain's colonization of the Subcontinent for bringing about "the greatest and, to speak the truth, the *only* social revolution ever heard of in Asia.... Whatever may have been the crimes of England, she was the unconscious tool of history in bringing about that revolution."[25] And of course Wright, as we have seen, retains this very unsentimental view of colonial hegemony in his views about the modernization of Africa. But that's kind of a side exhibit.

The Hastings prosecution found Burke ever mindful of the economics of colonialism, and it was through the cash venue that the horrors of the imperial venture would come home to corrupt the motherland: "We dread the operation of money. Do we not know that there are many men who wait, and who indeed hardly wait, the event of this prosecution, to let loose all the corrupt wealth of India, acquired by the oppression of that country, or the corruption of all the liberties of this." The currency of the realm would provide the circuit for colonial corruption to infiltrate the sovereign state. And even as his graphic imagery of torture and dismemberment fixed the species of colonial guilt, Burke implicated all of England in this economy of exploitation. The men of India, Burke maintained, "gave almost the whole produce of their labour to the East India Company: those hands which had been broken by persons under the Company's authority, produced to all England the comforts of their morning and evening tea."[26]

Allow me to quote further: "If their blood has not mingled extensively with yours, their labour power has long since entered your economic bloodstream. It is the sugar you stir, it is in the sinews of the infamous British sweet tooth, it is the tea leaves at the bottom of the British cuppa." Well put. Except these are, of course, the words of a latter-day rhizome—namely, Stuart Hall.[27] But more of this later.

Right now I want to pass on from this Burkean view of the economics of colonialism, to the second and third elements of the Burkean critique, though in fact they're pretty hard to decouple. I want to get a fix on what I'll call Burke's "relativizing imagination." For reasons that probably don't need explaining, it would be misleading simply to call Burke a relativist, but he was, in crucial respects, radically anti-foundationalist. (I guess most readers have figured out that I'm subjecting you to a semi-allegorical archaeology of British Cultural Studies generally, as well as contemporary colonial discourse theory particularly, which are the subject of Chapters 2 and 3. But it's still worth going through the motions. I think I can promise you that from now on, every single point I'm going to make is one that we can take home, that we can thread through any conversation about cultural resistance and cultural imperialism.)

A good test of this relativizing strain in Burke is provided by his response to Warren Hastings's principal line of defense. Hastings based his defense on the claims that his actions were justified by what he called "geographical ethics." Hastings (who knew very well the advantages of indirect rule) said—and you can see in this the ways that Hastings and Burke are really very similar, doppelgängers in a way, a fact that may help to explain Burke's near obsession with the man—that he believed that people should be governed according to native custom and that his actions were consistent with the mores of "Oriental Despotism." And yet Hastings was being tried in the House of Commons for offenses against British customary law.

Burke's response here is revealing: "I must do justice to the East, I must assert that their morality is equal to ours, in whatever regards the duties of governors, fathers, and superiors; and I challenge the world to show in any modern European book more true morality and wisdom than is to be found in the writings of Asiatic men in high trust. . . . If this be the true morality of Asia, as I affirm and can prove it is, the plea founded on Mr. Hastings's geographical morality is annihilated."

I want to emphasize the terms of argument here, which sound foundationalist but really aren't. Because rather than taking, as you might expect, recourse to a Kantian or Humean sort of universalizing or naturalizing morality, Burke at least provisionally accepted the validity of Hastings's construct. His counter-claim was that Hastings's assertion was empirically false: Burke said that he was acquainted with the mores of the region and that Hastings's behavior was in *contravention* of them. And note Burke's claim was not that Asia's morality was *identical* to England's; he said it was equal to England's, which is a claim of the same status as he might make about the respective civilizations.

This relativizing strain in Burke is, of course, precisely what won him round condemnation from the likes of James Mill, who claimed that Burke's morality boiled down to the proposal that whatever is, is right: "Every thing was to be protected; not, because it was good, but, because it existed."[28] And again, I don't want to play partisan history, but it's interesting to contrast Burke and Mill, author of *The History of British India*, who ridiculed the place as rude and barbarous and scoffed at its pretensions to antiquity. So Hastings and Burke—both of whom were profoundly learned in the actualities of Indian cultures—had more in common with each other than either did with Mill, the reformer and rationalizer. (And we also can contrast Burke's reverence for India's diverse traditions to Macaulay's famous remark that not even an Orientalist "could deny that a single shelf of a good European library was worth the whole native literature of India or Arabia.")[29]

You can get a feeling, if you spend too much time with the impeachment proceedings, that Hastings became Burke's detested brother discursively speaking, perhaps a smug Jacob to Burke's glowering Esau. You start to realize that precisely the same principles that motivated Burke's reverential anti-imperialism sponsored Hastings's villainy in equal measure. And it's hardly news that this relativist ethic, or rhetoric, which is ours, too, can raise problems that the anti-colonialist or "minority" intellectual has to come to terms with. The politics of oppositionality create a situation in which the claim for cultural authenticity, however it's framed, is always somehow legitimating, which is the whole subterranean moral argument behind the rhetoric deploring "cultural imperialism." (Baldwin mused, almost as an aside in his essay on the 1956 conference, that "it was not, now, the European necessity to go rummaging in the past, and through all the countries of the world, bitterly staking out claims to its cultural possessions.")[30] You can construct a moral fable where the figure of Warren Hastings takes on a life of its own. But more of that in the next chapter.

For what really attests to this strain in Burke is just this: Why did he need to spend eighteen years studying India? Why did he immerse himself in its "otherness" so obsessively? It makes no sense if you take Burke at his word that he was simply prosecuting one man and his associates for their legal transgressions, however heinous. It makes more sense if you take a closer look at Burke's own profound marginality.

"We submit to what we admire, but we love what submits to us." This might very well be an apothegm for our post-Freudian age, no doubt, but the words are Burke's.[31]

I don't want to dissolve the paradox that Burke the reactionary anti-Jacobin was also an eloquent champion of the oppressed—the wretched of the earth—the man who developed a compelling conception of the violence of cultural imperialism almost two centuries before it would be activated by modern ideologists of national liberation. That he was both a despiser and a supporter of the nobility, both a critic of capitalism and a proponent of the free market. That both his radicalism and his conservatism fed into each other, were operated by a shared logic.

Burke was, of course, an Irishman in England, born to a Catholic mother in an Anglican regime. Let's go further. He was also plagued with "hidden personal problems he would rather forget."[32] Burke would have retired from public life if he had not been tormented by "obscure vexations and contexts in the most private life," as he wrote to his childhood friend, Dick Shackleton.[33] Burke was a man dogged throughout his public career by rumors of homosexuality; cartoonists, combining religious and sexual stigmas, frequently depicted him as an effeminate Jesuit. And yet in 1870 (as Isaac Kramnick tells us), Burke stood up in the House of Commons to "protest the treatment of two homosexuals, Theodosius Reed and William Smith, who were sentenced, as part of their punishment for sodomy, to stand in the pillory for one hour. Smith died a victim of mob brutality." Horrified, Burke "spoke

eloquently in the House against this barbarity and secured a pension for Smith's widow."[34]

He took a stand, and he would suffer for it. *The
Morning Post* of April 13 wrote: "Every *man* applauds
the spirit of the spectators, and every *woman* thinks
their conduct right. It remained only for the patriotic
Mr. Burke to insinuate that the crime these men committed should not be held in the highest detestation."
Burke, the editorialist suggested, was neither man nor
woman. Rather, as later periodicals such as *Public Ad-
vertiser* would suggest, he was one of *them*, viz., a
"sodomist," or at least a sympathizer.

Now I'm taking the trouble to historicize this moment of gender and sexual identity in part because I
want to say more about it in the next chapter and the
way it comes to function in the symbolic economy
of imperialism. Burke's reading of colonialism was
highly sexualized (he figured Hastings as "this im-
petuous lover").[35] Many scholars have talked about
this, and it's always good to remember the uncanny
way in which issues of sexuality often enter in colonialist debates. More than that, though, I want to
complicate—or maybe forestall—a reading where,
for instance, here's a third world theory, but it's really
just Burke reconstructing and theorizing the alterity
of the periphery from the imperial center, and you

have this positional dichotomy already set in place. I want to insist on Burke's own marginality to the social order in which he was positioned; I want to insist on the otherness within Burke himself.

Now let's return to Burke's anti-foundationalism, which we can consider in isolation from his cultural obsessions. More abstractly, Burke wrote: "Metaphysical or physical speculations neither are, or ought to be, the Grounds of our Duties; because we can arrive at no certainty in them. They have a weight when they concur with our own natural feelings; very little when against them."[36] Although these are words that Stanley Fish or Richard Rorty would be perfectly happy to avow, they are obviously a refusal of the Enlightenment dream of foundations. Now Burke talked about foundations, or grounds, a great deal; he talked about human nature. But what you find is that the only foundations available to him were the aleatory sedimentations of history. All relations are contingent rather than necessary, and it's exactly this sense of the instability of our human identities that sponsored Burke's reactionary tendencies. Human nature, for Burke, is just another name for the human history, the natural history, of an individual.[37] And it accounts for his concern with custom and habit *because custom—culture, as a historical formation—was all there was.*

When our history is destroyed or expropriated, then we are, and I quote the mordant observation, "individuals without anchor, without horizon, colourless, stateless, rootless—a race of angels." Only these words are, of course, Frantz Fanon's.[38]

So let me recapitulate what I'm presenting as Burke's twin legacy. I want to figure it as an equilibrium equation, as in chemistry. On one side, we have Burke as the germinal theorist of anti-essentialism, of contingency, the anti-foundationalist for whom history exhausted the bases for social identity. I'm not claiming he was absolutely consistent in this, but I want to say this was a powerful current, and it was self-consciously advanced against the rationalist doxa.

Then on the other side, following as a consequence, are the veneration of settled, organic custom; the privileging of the extant; and something like a preservationist ethic, an assumption that there's something immanently valuable about cultures that leads us to respect their anteriority, their autonomy, and their integrity, instead of seeking their assimilation or extinction. (In self-reflexive form, at the very least, this can become conservatism.)

In Chapter 2, I want to puzzle through this almost dialectical pairing, through some of the tutelary figures of British Cultural Studies, and (this is where things start really getting interesting) through what happens when these twin jets are mobilized *against* the "long memory" and the notional community that British Cultural Studies took as its original object of study, which is to say, British culture. We'll find that the most recent challenge to what Michael Oakeshott calls rationalism comes from those who, like Burke, have a direct acquaintance with migrancy, diaspora, and displacement. It comes from the immigrant, from the migrant, from the most deracinated members of British society.

At the same time, Burke's tragic sense of history, his Christian pessimism, may accord with what Cornel West has famously described as the black prophetic tradition: "a form of Third World Left Romanticism" that "tempers its utopian impulse with the profound sense of the tragic character of life in history." One sees, West says, "a profound sense of the tragic linked to human agency that . . . is realistic enough not to project an excessive utopia."[39] Again, this is a strain, a conjunction of opposites, first articulated in Burke.

It strikes me that it's a sign of how reductively Burke has been read for so long that the phrase "Right Burkean" sounds like a pleonasm. But it isn't. I consider Michael Oakeshott, for example, a Right Burkean par excellence.[40] Like Richard Hoggart, the late

Raymond Williams, plainly, was a Left Burkean, and I think it's revealing of both the power and the limitations of Williams's work to consider him in that light. And that's not my act of positioning; it's his own. For the appropriation of Edmund Burke is the inaugural act of Raymond Williams's inaugural book, *Culture and Society*, a book that constructs a genealogy, a progressive British tradition, designed to encompass its author.[41] So we can see how overdetermined is Williams's decision to cast Burke in the originary position of temporal priority. It's not surprising that a symptomatic reading of Burke reveals all of the virtues and, equally, all of the tensions that run through Williams's own oppositional criticism and the really multifarious legacy of British Cultural Studies. I want to follow this through in my next chapter. But as Richard Wright would say, "The hour is late, Ladies and Gentlemen, and I am pressed for time."

CHAPTER TWO

Fade to Black:
From Cultural Studies
to Cultural Politics

Prologue

In the early 1990s, a lot of people were wondering why, when Cultural Studies was left for dead in its country of origin, we in the States jumped on it as the last best hope for humankind. I think Kobena Mercer reported a widespread sense of puzzlement when he complained that "for some reasons, there seems to be a lot of retroactive mythification going on; people talk about 'British Cultural Studies' as if . . . it were still at the center of the intellectual universe, whereas in Britain no one is particularly excited or interested in cultural studies anymore."[1] Now one might think that's just the story of the world, given the way ideas circulate. If structuralism is passé in its land of origin, then ship it, and it can have a new life across the channel, or across the Atlantic. Oscar Wilde once quipped that when good Americans die, they go to Paris. I think that in Paris, when good theories die, they go to America, to New Haven or Ithaca.

But I do want to resist the tempting model of "uneven development." So even though relations between critical communities here and in Britain really are curiously out of sync sometimes, I'm going to approach this admittedly fictitious unity of "Cultural Studies" in context, as it were, before discussing the uses for which it has been mobilized in the States since Mercer expressed his concern. We will, I hope, come to understand why rumors of its demise were greatly exaggerated, after all.

A Myth of Origins

In Chapter 1, I ventured that there's a sense in which British Cultural Studies began with the reappropriation of Edmund Burke, and I had a very specific reading in mind, the reading that opened Raymond Williams's first book, *Culture and Society*, published in 1958, a book that I first encountered while reading Tragedy with Williams in the English Department at Cambridge in 1974. (And at least here, I guess I'll join the consensus that Patrick Brantlinger reports when he argues that this book, "more than any other work, set the agenda for cultural studies in both Britain and America.")[2] Even as Richard Hoggart, author of *Uses of Literacy*, stands as the institutional founder of Cultural Studies, Raymond Williams, more than anyone else, serves intellectually as the tutelary spirit of this movement, its theoretical helmsman.

And Williams, inaugurating, as I said, that site of contestation called Cultural Studies, actually wrote very movingly about Burke. Williams took Burke to be a founding figure of the tradition of critical modernity and industrialization. He cited approvingly Matthew Arnold's comment that "almost alone in England, he brings thought to bear upon politics, he saturates politics with thought." And Williams continued:

> It is not "thought" in the common opposition to "feeling"; it is, rather, a special immediacy of experience, which works itself out, in depth, to a

particular embodiment of ideas that become, in themselves, the whole man. . . . Burke's writing is an articulated experience, and as such it has a validity which can survive even the demolition of its general conclusions. It is not that the eloquence survives where the cause has failed; the eloquence, if it were merely the veneer of a cause, would now be worthless. What survives is an experience, a particular kind of learning; the writing is important only to the extent that it communicates this. It is, finally, a personal experience become a landmark.[3]

I think that's a passage we can juxtapose to Michael Oakeshott if we want to trace that Burkean taproot, or rhizome. Williams's Burke "is one of that company of men who learn virtue from the margin of their errors, learn folly from their own persons. It is at least arguable that this is the most important kind of learning." He was a critic, first and foremost, of "economic individualism." Williams glossed Burke's remarks about "a people" in his *Reform of Representation in the House of Commons*—a text to which I return—as an assertion of the dependence on man's progress "not only on the historical community in the abstract sense, but on the nature of the particular community into which he has been born. No man can abstract himself from this; nor is it his alone to change." And here, finally, is Raymond Williams completing the transforming of Burke into a Marxist *avant la lettre*:

He prepared a position in the English mind from which the march of industrialism and liberalism was to be continually attacked. He established the idea of the State as the necessary agent of human perfection, and in terms of this idea the aggressive individualism of the nineteenth century was bound to be condemned. He established, further, the idea of what has been called an "organic society," where the emphasis is on the interrelation and continuity of human activities, rather than on the separation into spheres of interest, each governed by its own laws.

In Williams's view, the organic society of which Burke wrote was being tragically "broken up under his eyes by new economic forces,"[4] and even though Williams regretted Burke's blindnesses, he celebrated Burke's insights as germinal and empowering and produced him as the father of a counter-hegemonic tradition that is meant to culminate in the project that

Williams and a number of illustrious contemporaries were then, in disparate ways, pursuing.

The beginning of post-modernist wisdom came when the blindnesses and insights of this first generation of scholars came under question. Now Williams is, of course, an intellectual who underwent a process of continual reorientation. In a history of the Birmingham Centre that Stuart Hall gave in the mid-1970s, Hall carefully distinguished among Raymond Williams I, Raymond Williams II, Raymond Williams III, and so on.[5] (One reason Williams is a much more inescapable figure for us than Richard Hoggart, say, is that there never was a Hoggart the second or third; certainly Williams's theoretical openness was all the more remarkable by contrast.) But there are continuities among change, and it's important to see that Williams inherited both sides of the Burkean equation: not merely the recognition of the contingency of culture and identity,[6] but also, and more problematically, a reverence toward "settled custom."[7] (In fact, if you think back to Karl Marx's famous remark that "the traditions of all dead generations weigh like a nightmare on the brains of the living," you can see that Williams's usual invocation of "tradition" had more of a Burkean inflection than a Marxian one.)

And attention began to be focused on this problem about twenty-five years or so after the publication of *Culture and Society*. People began to scrutinize Williams's reliance on the notion of a "common culture," on the historical rootedness of the English working man, on the valorization of "lived identities formed through long experience and actual sustained social relations"—the whole right hand of the Burkean equation, in short.[8] Writing in 1983, for example, Williams advanced a seemingly organicist conception of culture based on ethno-territorial continuity: "The real history of the peoples of these islands . . . goes back . . . to the remarkable society of the Neolithic shepherds and farmers, and back beyond them to the hunting peoples who did not simply disappear but are also amongst our ancestors."[9]

But if this is the "real history," it follows that some of us—those not numbered among the possessive collectivity "our ancestors"—must not be Britain's "real people." The passage reprises the Anglo-Saxonist myths of lineage that serve to buttress an exclusionary and imperialist ideology of "Englishness." (Remember, this is a country where in the 1950s Winston Churchill could suggest to Harold Macmillan that if the Conservative Party wanted to win elections, it should adopt the slogan "Keep England

White.")[10] Pioneering publications from the Birmingham Centre such as *The Empire Strikes Back* (1982) strove to foreground issues that were previously subsumed or subordinated within "larger" structures of analysis.

Paul Gilroy's germinal critique, in *There Ain't No Black in the Union Jack* (1987), is worth quoting at length because as a minority critique of the provincialism of the English left, it has become a standard point of reference in subsequent debates: "Williams's arguments effectively deny that blacks can share a significant 'social identity' with their white neighbours, who, in contrast to more recent arrivals, inhabit what Williams calls 'rooted settlements' articulated by 'lived and formed identities.' . . . Williams's discussion of 'race' and nation . . . is notable for its refusal to examine the concept of racism which has its own historic relationship with ideologies of Englishness, Britishness, and national belonging." That part of Gilroy's arguments sticks in the knife. Let's resume: "Quite apart from Williams's apparent endorsement of the presuppositions of the new racism, the strategic silences in his work contribute directly to its strength and resilience. The image Williams has chosen to convey his grasp of 'race' and nation, that of a resentful English working man, intimidated by the alterity of his alien neighbors is . . . redolent of other aspects of modern Conservative racism and nationalism."[11]

This part of the argument *twists* the knife. It links Williams's success as a public intellectual to his ideological failures; Williams's discourse is seen as substantially continuous with Enoch Powell's. And what Gilroy's critique inaugurated was, in a sense, a changing of the guard, a theoretical realignment that would not be confined to the classroom.

Not confined, either, to immediate concerns of minority critics. From Robert Young, editor of the *Oxford Literary Review*, we hear the charge that the usual notion of culture in contemporary theory is "a Burkean notion"—a phrase he uses, of course, in the conventionally pejorative sense—and the counsel to

> distance the concept of "culture" from its authenticating association with the work of Raymond Williams. It is important to recall that the idea of a cultural politics was in fact invented by non-Europeans, such as Fanon or Mao, as a means for resisting forms of colonial and neo-colonial political power; it was itself the product of a recognition of the inadequacy of the traditional categories invoked in the European arena to effect political

change. Its adoption in Europe, however, has tended to be limited to an identification of cultural phenomena with pre-established political positions.[12]

In the end, Young argues, this sort of cultural politics only repeats "the very same inside/outside structure of racism that is constitutive of English Literature itself." Citing *The Empire Strikes Back*, Young asserts that "those working at the Birmingham Centre for Contemporary Cultural Studies have already demonstrated the extent to which cultural study and neo-colonialism are intertwined."[13] The irony of his proposal is arresting: Cultural studies must and will be dismantled—and where are the agents of this dismantlement to be found? Why, in the Birmingham Centre for Contemporary Cultural Studies, of course.

Williams was, for his part, discomfited by the identity politics he associated with—and these are his words—"many minority liberals and socialists, and especially those who by the nature of their work or formation are themselves nationally and internally mobile." In other words: not settled, not truly English, not truly part of the nation. He was uncomfortable with identity politics, but he was shrewd enough to note its emergence, to note that the "long memory" was now threatened by a post-essentialist politics of identity that exalted a vision of migrancy, hybridity, exile, creolization: all the elements of what would come to be celebrated as a "diaspora aesthetics."[14]

Fade to Black

It would be reductive to figure this critique as a "generational shift"; the influence of many of the seminal figures—Dick Hebdige and Stuart Hall, for example—crosses over generations. But there *is* a rupture here. As Benita Parry has written about the development of Cultural Studies, "Just how far the study of the cultural situation in Britain has travelled from its beginnings in Anglocentric Cultural Studies concerned to recuperate the hidden histories of autochthonous subjected peoples . . . is marked by [Kobena] Mercer's account of the contemporary aesthetic as a process of critically appropriating and 'creolizing' elements from the master codes of the dominant culture."[15] And in the process, the real vitality of Cultural Studies did not so much die as fade to black.

Stuart Hall's very liminality makes him an intriguing figure here, and in quite a number of ways. As a mentoring presence across successive generations, he provides the continuity between the hard-won insights of the British Cultural Studies represented by Williams and Hoggart, whom he succeeded as head of the Birmingham Centre, and the new black British cultural workers. (For reasons that I have never been able to ascertain, when I was a first-year student in English at Cambridge, stumbling my way through practical criticism and cultural theory, trying to work out a theory of race and superstructure, as it were, Williams never once mentioned to me that Hall was black, if he mentioned his work at all.) If Cultural Studies is notoriously a site of contestation rather than coalescence, Hall's generosity of vision allows him to adopt a stand that is accommodative rather than antagonistic toward many of his compeers on the British left. I once wrote that the one defining feature of the true intellectual is that his primary animus is directed against *other* intellectuals. And one of the reasons you really have to admire Hall is that he's an exception to that dismal rule. At the same time, the fact that he eschews grand theory for a vision of theory that is always local and provisional can make it easy for Americans to underestimate the value of his contributions, and I want to get to that in a bit.

But I want to stress the *departure* entailed by his call to separate the concept of ethnicity from "an equivalence with nationalism, imperialism, racism, and the state." This proves one of the enabling gestures for a post-essentialist recuperation of identity. The problem with the post-structuralist critiques of ethnic absolutism was that they quickly led to a sort of post-modern universalism that foreclosed the possibility of a politics of identity. Stuart Hall's reinstatement of "ethnicity" is meant to counter-balance this tendency. It's equally important to notice that the right hand of the Burkean equation by no means falls by the wayside.

Here, again, is Paul Gilroy, describing the "traditions" that the blacks who have arrived in Britain since World War II have "brought with them." In the colonial state, he sees "the dying embers of the furnace in which their now-transplanted political consciousness was forged. They and their British born children have preserved organic links with it, in their kitchens and temples—in their *communities*."

Williams's rhetoric of lineage, organicity, and community in blackface? Perhaps, but all blackface is not equal. Williams's valorization of community and generational links was never jettisoned; it was merely pluralized. Gilroy wants to emphasize that the word "radical" contains the idea of rootedness. (I'll only remark, in passing, the point of departure here for

those who *do* want to retreat from this rhetoric—
Homi Bhabha, for example—and supplant it with
the imagery of liminality, migrancy, monadic and
nomadic dispersion. I'm inclined to downplay this
split because in practice it seems largely to be a matter
of accentuation. The currently privileged term "diaspora aesthetics" is meant, I think, to accommodate
both monadic and communitarian rhetorics,[16] which
is only to say that it preserves both sides of the
Burkean equation, so that it's the enabling tension
that appears to run through all diasporic and post-
colonial criticism.)

And few people have negotiated between these
two registers more nimbly than Hall. I mean, this is
the dilemma of post-modern activism, and he ac-
knowledges that. "You tend to fall into a hole," he
writes. "Is it possible, acknowledging the discourse
of self-reflexivity, to constitute a politics in the recognition of the necessarily fictional nature of the modern self, and necessary arbitrariness of the closure
around the imaginary communities in relation to
which we are constantly in the process of becoming
'selves'?" An overemphasis on the contingency of culture can be a problem. As he writes, "The politics of
infinite dispersal is the politics of no action at all: and
one can get into that from the best of all possible mo-

tives (i.e., from the highest of all possible intellectual abstractions.")[17] Following Ernesto Laclau's revision of Antonio Gramsci, Hall's response is to call for a "politics of articulation" in the stead of one based on integral selves, based on necessary correspondence between one thing and another.[18] Hall wants us "not only to speak the language of dispersal, but also the language of, as it were, contingent closures of articulation." And Stuart Hall's promulgation of this, the new common sense, is always an act of balancing: "Ethnicity *can* be a constitutive element in the most viciously regressive kind of nationalism or national identity. But in our times, as in an imaginary community, it is also beginning to carry some other means, and to define a new space for identity. . . . But it is not necessarily armour plated against other identities. It is not tied to fixed, permanent, unalterable oppositions. It is not wholly defined by exclusion."

But there's also a richer, more personal vein in Hall that deserves attention as well. The imperative to acknowledge one's own positionality is no mere theoretical abstraction for him. Hall tells us that he left Jamaica for England "to get away from my mother."[19] Edmund Burke, as we know from his private correspondence, left Ireland to get away from his abusive father. In 1757 (he was in his late twenties,

long before his Indian obsession), Burke met an expatriate Indian in London and introduced himself:
"Edmund Burke, at your service. I am a runaway son
from a father, as you are."[20] If his ostensible referent
is to their respective nations, we know, too, that the
ambivalence of *familial* exile, *familial* alienation, clings
fast to that of geographical displacement, a fact that
so many of our finest novelists of migrancy have explored. Sara Suleri's memoir *Meatless Days* (1987) is
a very moving example. (When Burke was sixteen,
he wrote, "The only way to be safe is to be silent."
Only later were his "colonized" silences about his own
sexuality, nationality, ethnicity, and religion transformed into a torrential flood of words on a colonized
exteriority.)

The act of self-positioning was obviously extremely important for Richard Hoggart and Raymond
Williams. What Hall is demonstrating is that this
doesn't need to be a purely celebratory act. Hall insists, rightly, on distinguishing between a conception
of identity founded in an archaeology—in the sense
of *res gestae*—and one produced by a narrative, even
if an archaeological narrative. For him, that "partnership of past and present" is always an "imaginary
reunification."[21] But he also insists—something forgotten too quickly in the post-modernist urge to exalt

indeterminacy—that "cultural identities come from somewhere, have histories." In one of his nicest *aperçus*, he writes that "identities are the names we give to the different ways we are positioned by, and position ourselves in, the narratives of the past."

I like that. It says that our social identities represent our sense of imbrications in an historical narrative. But I think Hall senses there's a delicate balance to be struck, which is why in the essay I'm citing, he develops the point far beyond the simple requirements of propositional exposition, stating and restating his position.[22] His analysis of the precariousness of identity is, of course, fully Burkean, even though his attitude toward that instability is insouciant where Burke was fearful. And his sense of difference within identity is a sense that lived experience, that personal history, has conferred on him as it did on Burke.

Hall asserts that the history of the colonized is—as Burke feared—irretrievable. He proposes, as Burke could not, an imaginative reconstruction, and there's a distinctly voluntarist strain in Hall at this point.[23] I say this not by way of criticism but of praise. Because it's really the voluntarist strain in a theorist like Hall that's pointed a way from Cultural Studies to cultural politics in England and, in particular, the cultural renascence in black Britain, which began in the 1980s and has lasted far longer than either the Harlem Renaissance or the Black Arts Movement in the sixties (both of which lasted less than a decade) and has achieved in Rivington Place a form of institutionalization of cultural retrieval that neither movement could have imagined, let alone realized, for themselves.

Only in England

Stuart Hall gets in a London taxicab one day. The driver thinks he recognizes Hall from his lectures on television. They begin to chat. Hall had devoted considerable effort to raising matching funds in response to a grant of £5.9 million from the Arts Council England Lottery Capital 2 program. Despite valiant effort, he had not had much luck. He chats with the driver about this project, which he and his colleagues want to call "Rivington Place," musing aloud about realizing his dream of building Britain's "first permanent public space, dedicated to the education of the public in culturally diverse visual arts and photography in the UK," as the Web site will put it. He tells the driver that the Arts Council has given a generous grant but that the grant is dependent upon raising matching funds. The driver casually mentions that his daughter works for Barclays Bank's corporate sponsorship department. The rest is history: Barclays contributes £1.1 million toward the project, becoming Rivington Place's founding corporate partner. Two visual arts organizations that emerged out of the radical Black Arts Movement of the late 1980s, with a decidedly left-wing orientation, win a grant from the government lottery to build Britain's first permanent, publicly funded gallery dedicated to the exhibition and preservation of the black and multicultural arts, and secure a matching grant of £1.1 million from one of the bastions of international corporate capitalism. To paraphrase Don King, that indefatigable champion of the American flag and our free markets, this outcome, abundant in irony, would be possible only in England.

Rivington Place, located in London's East End, is a magnificent art gallery and library, the latter named in honor of Stuart Hall, designed by David Adjaye. It is the home of Autograph ABP (founded in 1988 by David A. Bailey, Rotimi Fani-Kayode, and others) and Iniva, the Institute for International Visual Arts (founded in 1994, both funded by the Arts Council England). Its opening in October 2007 stood as visually eloquent testimony to one of the primary differences between the renaissance of the black arts in Harlem (primarily a literary movement) and the renaissance of black arts in Britain (primarily a movement based on the visual arts, including film, and cultural theory). Both were movements of cultural retrieval, but the latter benefited enormously from studying, and avoiding, certain wrong turns taken by its American antecedent, which it grounded itself against and sometimes even formally riffed or signified upon as a central part of its mission of cultural retrieval.

For the practice of cultural retrieval—tempered with a sense of its lability, its contingency, its constructedness—has sponsored a remarkable time of black creativity in Britain, or as we are bidden to call it, "cultural production," since the early 1980s. And in no genre has more astonishingly accomplished work been produced than in the work of recent black British film collectives, such as Akomfrah's Black Audio Film Collective, which really can be seen to have deepened and expanded the critical insights of a Stuart Hall, a Paul Gilroy, or a Homi K. Bhabha in a refreshingly fecund and dialectic manner that simply did not occur in the Harlem Renaissance. This hasn't been a relation of mirroring between theory and practice, but rather a rare relation of productive dialogue. Renaissance writers and critics reacted to each other, of course, but primarily in a relation of thesis to antithesis. In Britain, theory shaped the forms of practice, and practice, in turn, shaped theories of practice. We can see this clearly in the work of Isaac Julien, as one example among many.

Looking for Modernism

So I want to talk a little about one film in particular, which may be the best known of the genre in the States, Isaac Julien's *Looking for Langston*, which is a Sankofa production, and the way it sets history, identity, and desire in very serious play. To me, it's no accident that *Looking for Langston* is, in part, a meditation on the Harlem Renaissance. Distance and displacement have their benefits, as the literature of migrancy reminds us, so it isn't altogether surprising that one of the most provocative and insightful reflections on the Harlem Renaissance and the cultural politics of black America should come from across the Atlantic. I want to take a look at black New York from the standpoint of black London. I want to examine the relationship between a New York–based cultural movement, such as it was, in the 1920s and one in London in the 1980s. Of course, the question of modernism has always also been one of a cultural vanguard or elite. And that means that the old "burden of representation" is always present. "The ordinary Negroes hadn't heard of the Negro Renaissance," Langston Hughes remarked ruefully. "And if they had, it hadn't raised their wages any."[24] Always, there is the question, What have you done for us?

But to see *Looking for Langston* as an act of historical reclamation, we might begin with the retheorizing of identity politics in black British Cultural Studies, among such critics and theorists as Hall, Gilroy, Hazel Carby, and Kobena Mercer. Again, in Hall's conception, our social identities represent the way we participate in an historical narrative; our histories may be irretrievable, but they invite imaginative reconstruction. In this spirit, diasporic feminist critics such as Carby have made the call for a "usable past." I'm talking, of course, about the work of the black British film collectives, which really can be seen to have deepened and expanded these arguments. Again, this has not been a relation of mirroring, but of productive dialogue.

To talk about the way *Looking for Langston* sets in play history, identity, and desire, start with the fact that *Looking for Langston* is avowedly a meditation on the Harlem Renaissance. And let me emphasize that historical particularity is an essential part of the film's texture, rather splendidly realized, I think, by Derek

Brown, the film's art director. Throughout the film, archival footage, including film extracts from Oscar Micheaux and period footage of Bessie Smith's "St. Louis Blues," is interspersed with Nina Kellgren's cinematography. What I want to argue is that the film's evocation of the historical Harlem Renaissance is, among other things, a self-reflexive gesture; there's a relation, even a typology, established between black British cinema of the 1980s and the cultural movement of the 1920s that we call the Harlem Renaissance. By the choice of subject, the film brings out, in a very self-conscious way, the analogy between this contemporary ambit of black creativity and a historical present.

We look for Langston, but we discover Isaac. It's an association that's represented quite literally in one of the opening images of the film, where the film's director makes his sole appearance in front of the camera. He is the corpse in the casket. With six mourners presiding, Hughes's wake is a black-tie affair. And, of course, the film is also an act of mourning, in memoriam to three men who died in 1987: Bruce Nugent, James Baldwin, and Joseph Beam. ("This nut might kill us," we hear Essex Hemphill say in one sequence, reflecting on the AIDS epidemic. "This kiss could turn to stone.")

Visually, as I mentioned, there's a circulation of images between the filmic present and the archival past. Textually, something of the same interplay is enacted, with poetry and prose from Bruce Nugent ("Smoke, Lilies and Jade," which receives perhaps the most elaborate and affecting *tableau vivant* in the film), Langston Hughes (including selections from "The Negro Artist and the Racial Mountain," *The Big Sea, Montage of a Dream Deferred*, and other works), James Baldwin (from *The Price of the Ticket*), an essay by critic and journalist Hilton Als, and six poems by Essex Hemphill. We hear an interchange of different voices, different inflections, different accents, including Hall reading expository prose of Als, Hughes reading his own work, Toni Morrison reading Baldwin, and Erick Ray Evans reading Nugent. The credits include Hall's as the "British voice," an interestingly ambiguous formulation. The result is an interlacement of past and present, the blues, jazz, Motown, and contemporary dance music, London and New York: a trans-temporal dialogue on the nature of identity and desire and history.

But the typology to which the film is devoted also enables another critique of the identity politics we've inherited from the black nationalism of our youth, a critique that focuses on a malign sexual politics. Like the self-proclaimed "aesthetic movement" of England's yellow 1890s, chronicled by Arthur Symonds, parodied by Robert Hitchens, and promulgated by such "born antinomians" as Oscar Wilde, Alfred Douglas, and Lionel Johnson, the Harlem Renaissance was in fact a handful of people. The usual roll call would invoke figures such as Langston Hughes, Claude McKay, Alain Locke, Countee Cullen, Wallace Thurman, and Bruce Nugent—which is to say that it was surely as gay as it was black, not that it was exclusively either of these things.

Yet this, in view of its emblematic importance to later movements of black creativity in this country, is what makes the powerful current of homophobia in black letters a matter of particular interest and concern. If *Looking for Langston* is a meditation on the Harlem Renaissance, it is equally an impassioned rebuttal to the virulent homophobia associated with the Black Power and Black Aesthetic movements in the sixties. On this topic, the perfervid tone that Eldridge Cleaver adopted toward Baldwin—to whom *Looking for Langston* is dedicated—indicates only a sense of what was perceived to be at stake in policing black male sexuality. We see the same obsession running through the early works of Sonia Sanchez, and, of course, Amiri Baraka. "Most American White men are trained to be fags," he wrote in the essay collection *Home*. "For this reason it is no wonder their faces are weak and blank, left without the hurt that reality makes."[25] Amid the racial battlefield, a line was drawn, but it was drawn on the shifting sands of sexuality. To cross that line, Baraka told us, would be an act of betrayal. And it is worth noting that, at least in a literal sense, the film opens in the year 1967, with the death of Langston Hughes and the playing of a Riverside radio program in memoriam.

It is difficult to read Baraka's words today: "without the hurt that reality makes." Baldwin once remarked that being attacked by white people only made him flare hotly into eloquence; being attacked by black people, he confessed, made him want to break down and cry. Baldwin hardly emerged from the efflorescence of his black nationalism in the 1960s unscathed. Baldwin and Beam could both have told LeRoi Jones a great deal about the "hurt that reality makes," as could a lot of black gay men in Harlem today who are tired of being used for batting practice. And in the wake of a rising epidemic of physical violence against gays, violence of the sort that Melvin Dixon has affectingly depicted in his novel *Vanishing Rooms*—it's difficult to say that we have progressed since LeRoi Jones.

That's not to say that the ideologues of black nationalism in this country have any unique claim on homophobia. But it is an almost obsessive motif that runs through the major authors of the Black Aesthetic and the Black Power movements. In short, national identity became sexualized in the 1960s in such a way as to engender a curious subterranean connection between homophobia and nationalism. It's important to confront this head on to make sense of the ways *Looking for Langston* both fosters and transcends a kind of identity politics.

Surely one of the salient features of the work is its attitude toward the corporeal, the way in which the black body is sexualized. Gloria Watkins has noted that Nina Kellgren's camera presents the black male body as vulnerable, soft, even passive, in marked contrast to its usual representation in American film. This is a way of disrupting a visual order, a hardened convention of representation. There's a scene in which we see slides of Robert Mapplethorpe photos projected on a backdrop while a white man walks through them. And I think there's a tacit contrast between those images, with their marmoreal surfaces and primitivist evocations, and Kellgren's own vision of masculinity unmasked. Indeed, this may be the film's most powerful assault on the well-policed arena of black masculinity. "*And soft,*" Nugent writes of his character Beauty, "*soft*" (my italics).[26]

In short, by insistently foregrounding—and then refiguring—issues of gender and desire, filmmakers such as Reece Auguiste, Maureen Blackwood, and Isaac Julien are engaged in an act of both cultural retrieval and reconstruction. And the historicity of that act—the way it takes form as a search for a usable past—is, as Hazel Carby and Houston Baker show, entirely characteristic of diasporic culture.

So the dialogue with the past, even a past figured as nonrecuperable, turns out to be a salient feature of what might be called the Black London Renaissance. The partnership of past and present is recast across the distances of exile, through territories of the imagination and of space.

A film like *Looking for Langston* is able to respond to the hurtfully exclusionary obsessions of the black nationalist moment, and our own cultural moment as well, by constructing a counter-history in which desire and mourning and identity can interact in their full complexity, but in a way that registers the violence of history. So there are two reductive ways of viewing the film. The first is preoccupied with fixing the historical questions about Hughes's sex life. The second says that the film is an imaginative meditation and that "real" history is completely immaterial to it. On their own, both approaches are misguided. A more instructive approach is emblematized nicely by the Akan figure of *sankofa* itself (the word literally means "go back and retrieve it"), which refers to the figure of a bird with its head turned backward: again, the partnership of past and present. Obviously, the film isn't positivist history, and yet history, and the status of history, are its immediate concerns. So we need to take seriously what Kobena Mercer calls the "artistic commitment to archaeological inquiry" that's at work and at play here.[27] And, of course, Hall's insistence that "cultural identities come from somewhere, have histories," is very much to the point.

Hall's involvement is, of course, audible in this film, and I mean that literally: We hear his voice on the soundtrack; we hear him reading poetry, thereby becoming a more than theoretical presence in the film. (And this literal insertion of the theorist into the practice isn't uncommon in these films: In a Black Audio Film Collective production *Twilight City* (1989), directed by Reece Auguiste, Homi Bhabha remembers that the one thing that struck him when he first went to London as a boy was the absence of smell; he thought his nose had died.) In Julien's film, we hear an enmeshment of the poetry of Langston

Hughes with that of Essex Hemphill, among others, establishing that trans-temporal dialogue to which I referred previously, a discursive intercourse, on the nature of identity and desire and history.

Although the film is not a simple exercise in identity politics, it cannot dispense with the moment of narcissism, of self-recognition. Hence the use of the mirror tableaux that thematize the film critic's concern with the dialectic of identification and spectatorship. A man in a club sees himself in the mirror and is caught up short. Water—ponds and puddles—is used as a reflecting surface. Indeed, toward the film's end we are presented with a series of men who lie, Narcissus-like, with their faces to a reflective surface. A belated version of the Lacanian mirror stage? Self-recognition? Or something else entirely? In the prose poem "The Disciple," Oscar Wilde writes:

When Narcissus died the pool of his pleasure changed from a cup of sweet waters into a cup of salt tears, and the Oreads came weeping through the woodland that they might sing to the pool and give it comfort.

. . . "We do not wonder that you should mourn in this manner for Narcissus, so beautiful was he."

"But was Narcissus beautiful?" said the pool. . . .
"I loved Narcissus because, as he lay on my banks
and looked down at me, in the mirror of his eyes
I saw ever my own beauty mirrored."

The film, remember, is called *Looking for Langston*; it does not promise he will be found. In fact, I think that *Looking for Langston* leads us away from the ensolacement of identity politics, the simple exaltation of identity. We are to go behind the mirror, as Wilde urged. The film gives us angels—there are six of them, including musician Jimmy Somerville, with wings of netting and wire—but they are fallen angels, as Hemphill tells us. There are moments of carnival—a club with spirited dancing amid the smashing of champagne glasses—but there are no utopias here. An angel holds a photograph of Langston Hughes, of James Baldwin, but history remains in the phrase that Hall repeats: "the smiler with the knife." The carnival is disrupted by a group of men who are described indifferently by the credits as "thugs and police" and who present both the authority of the state and the skinhead malevolence that is its funhouse reflection. In films like *Looking for Langston*, Cultural Studies becomes cultural work.

The Politics of Representation

At the same time, the controversy that surrounds the production of Sankofa and Black Audio, the two most prominent collectives, leads to what has become *the* central problem for cultural criticism in our day. It's a theoretical terrain that can be taken as either a gold mine or a minefield, depending on your point of view. I speak of the "new politics of representation" and the way this impinges on the normative self-image of the so-called oppositional intellectual.

To the extent that black British cinema is represented as an act of cultural politics, it then becomes vulnerable to a political reproach as elitist, Europeanized, overly highbrow. As a black cultural product without a significant black audience, its very blackness becomes suspect.

This line of reproach ought to ring a bell: As I suggested at the start, it reprises one of the oldest debates in the history of African American letters, which is usually framed as the Responsibilities of the Negro Artist. But the populist critique always operates in tandem as a statement about artists and critics.

The centrality of the issue is shown in the fact that a synoptic manifesto on the new politics of representation was issued jointly by Isaac Julien and Kobena Mercer.[28] Their argument follows Paul

Gilroy, Pierre Bourdieu, and Ernesto Laclau—and a certain eighteenth-century political theorist named Edmund Burke—in linking a critique of essentialism to a critique of the paradigm of representation as delegation.

It's been argued that we should supplant the vanguardist paradigm of "representation" with the "articulation of interests." In such a way can we lighten the "burden of representation," even if we cannot dispense with it. But whose interest is being articulated?

Worrying that independent black British cinema has become too estranged from the black community, Gilroy has recently proposed what he calls "populist modernism"—which some have decried as a highbrow version of the NAACP Image Awards. There are worries that normative proposals such as populist modernism can become techniques for policing artistic boundaries, for separating the collaborationist sheep from the oppositional goats, or perhaps the other way around. Gilroy cites Richard Wright's *The Outsider* as a model for black art, but the poetic career of Langston Hughes might be an even more appropriate candidate for the category.

Perhaps more than any other African American artist in the last century, Hughes was elected popularly to serve as our "Representative Negro," the poet of his race, just as Frederick Douglass had been known as the "Representative Colored Man in the United States" in the century before. As we know, the burden of representation bore heavily upon him, profoundly shaping his career and preoccupations, propelling and restraining his own involvement with literary modernism. Nor is it surprising that this image should be, even in our own day, subject to censorship and restriction. Julien's difficulties with acquiring the rights to Hughes's texts reflect, in an ironic way, the central argument of his film.

How "modernist" is Julien's own technique? Manthia Diawara, a leading intellectual champion of black British cinema, has observed that *Looking for Langston* has evident affinities with many avant-garde and experimental films of the 1970s. And yet, he argues, the film "appropriates the forms of avant-garde cinema not for mere inclusion in the genre, but in order to redefine it by changing its content, and re-ordering its formal disposition."[29] In Julien's hands, Diawara suggests, the techniques of the avant-garde are made to "reveal that which the genre itself represses."[30] Nor is it an uncritical act of reclamation. Diawara notes that "the dependency of artists and writers of the Renaissance upon their white patrons, and the links between the movement and the Modernist Primitivism, are revealed in *Looking for Langston* as moments of ambiguity and ambivalence."[31]

Indeed, the importance of open textured films like *Looking for Langston* is in presenting an aesthetics that can embrace ambiguity. Perhaps *Looking for Langston* is not without its reverential moments, but neither is it a work of naïve celebration. It presents an identitarian history as a locus of discontinuities and affinities, of shared pleasures and perils. Perhaps the real achievement of this film is not simply that it rewrites the history of African-American modernism, but also that it compels its audiences to participate in the rewriting.

The strictures of "representation" have had wide and varied permutations in the black community. For as we know, the history of African Americans is marked by noble demands for political tolerance from the larger society, but also by a paradoxical tendency to censure our own. W. E. B. Du Bois was rebuked by the NAACP for his nationalism in the 1930s and then again for his socialism a decade or so later. James Baldwin and Ralph Ellison were victims of the Black Arts Movement in the 1960s, the former for his sexuality, the latter for his insistence upon individualism. Martin Luther King and Eartha Kitt, strange bedfellows at best, were roundly condemned for their early protests against the Vietnam War. Amiri Baraka repudiated a whole slew of writers in the 1960s for being too "assimilationist," then invented a whole new canon of black targets when he became a Marxist a few years later. Michele Wallace, Ntozake Shange, and Alice Walker have been called black male-bashers and accused of calculated complicity with white racists. Not surprisingly, many black intellectuals are acutely aware of the hazards of falling out of favor with the thought police, whether in whiteface or black.

So the very newest generation of black British cultural critics are brave, resourceful, and dialectical when they seek to recuperate everything that was *right* about the 1960s movements of ethnicist self-affirmation. I can't pass over without comment the irony that even as the veterans and children and grandchildren of the American Black Arts Movement turn to black Britain to retheorize, at last, the vexed concept of ethnicity, the children of the black Britain diaspora are returning to the 1960s to recuperate usable models for the present. And that's the *historical* significance of the fact that Mercer once gave a paper called "1968: Periodizing Postmodern Politics and Identity." It marks the incorporation of the 1960s into that identitarian trajectory: an acknowledgment of another viable resource for cultural retrieval. Bury the body, and your kids will dig it up. (However slapdash, Ivory Keenan Wayan's *I'm Gonna Get You Sucka* can at least be appreciated as an instantiation of Karl Marx's famous line about the reprise of historical events: the first time as tragedy; the second, as farce.) And so the 1960s are retrieved under the auspices of the postmodern post-essentialist exaltation of contingency and indeterminacy without, however, the apocalyptic sounds that marked the decade's inception. The 1960s tragedians will survive, if they survive, as players in a farce—a farce of racial perversions and sexual obsessions and (apologies to Coco Fusco) wet dreams of oppositionality.[32] And as academicians, we have, all of us, been cast in an especially unrewarding role in that farce: The academic, naturally, must play the straight man, the straight man to history.

Reforming Representation

I promised earlier that we'd be returning to Burke's speech on a "Motion to Reform Representation," and I'm a man of my word. In 1988, Julien and Mercer recast the debate about black representation by focusing on the tension "between representation as a practice of depicting and representation as a practice of delegation. Representational democracy, like the classic realist text, is premised on an implicitly mimetic theory of representation as correspondence with the 'real.'"[33]

Now, I just said that there was a connection between a post-essentialist identity politics (culled from Gramsci, culled from creative exegetes such as Laclau) and the politics of representation. Laclau makes the connection explicit: You can't stop with the dispersion of the integral subject, because that entails the contingency of all social relations, so that the very notion of a "social formation" goes overboard, and the notion of the political representation of interests as transparency can no longer be taken for granted. In Chapter 1, I read Burke as anticipating the "contingency of the self," the contingency of all social relations, now lodged at the heart of all our postmodern theories, and his take on the nature of political representation followed that logic.

Laclau and Mouffe observe, "Now, every relation of representation is founded on a fiction: that of the presence at a certain level of something which, strictly speaking, is absent from it."[34] Their political analysis seeks to supplant what they describe as "the *fictio iuris* of representation" and what Burke dismissed as a "legal fiction." Amid eighteenth-century debates over the nature of representational democracy, Burke asserted that true political representation is impossible the minute it involves delegation, the moment we have the separation of the represented from the representative: the moment, that is, it becomes a relation of *representation*. With Burke's anti-foundationalist skepticism of what he called "the fairy wand of philosophy," he spoke instead of "prescription," where Laclau would employ a vocabulary of "hegemonic articulation." ("The House of Commons is a legislative body corporate by prescription, not made upon any given theory, but existing prescriptively.")[35] And we might wonder if the intersection here of Burke and our latter-day post-Marxists can't be construed as a shared conversation on the ramifications of contingency.

So, should we supplant the vangardist paradigm of representation with the "articulation of interests," as some have argued? It's a counter-model meant to deny any natural relation of synecdoche. Yet this model allows us to articulate these relations, to clean a space for the model of populist modernism as a self-conscious practice of articulation. Gilroy and Mercer famously debated the issue of populist modernism, but it's worth pointing out that there was no point of factual or theoretical disagreement in their respective positions.[36]

Gilroy proposes populist modernism as a possible modality of the articulation of interests and cites Richard Wright's *The Outsider* as the novel in which

this doctrine is "most cogently expressed." It's interesting that nowhere is Wright being read more atten-
tively today than in Britain or more creatively than
by Gilroy in his highly influential book *The Black Atlantic*.[37] Gilroy finds Wright valuable as a model for
ethnicist affirmation tempered with a materialist ap-
prehension. He's seen, in words I quoted in my previous chapter, as one of the few black writers who saw
"black nationalism as a beginning rather than an end."
Part of what's fascinating about Gilroy's appropriation
of Wright is that it becomes a theory about the dis-
empowering effects of theory. This Richard Wright,
as reconstituted for Cultural Studies, asks us to accept
the "nationalist implications of our lives" and calls for
"a nationalism that knows its origins, its limitations;
and is aware of the dangers in its positions."[38]

I submit that a nationalism shorn of idealist illusions, a nationalism that knows its origins and limitations, is no nationalism at all. It is *Hamlet* without
the Prince of Denmark. As Kwame Anthony Appiah
has observed about the construction of collective
identities in general, "The demands of agency may
entail a misrecognition of its genesis."[39] A sense of
this is poignantly dramatized in Frantz Fanon's dialogue with Jean-Paul Sartre. Reading Sartre's account
of Négritude (as an antithesis preparatory to a "soci-

ety without races," hence "a transition and not a conclusion"), Fanon reported in his justly celebrated essay "The Fact of Blackness," "I felt I had been robbed of my last chance. . . . A consciousness committed to experience is ignorant, has to be ignorant, of the essences and the determinations of its being. . . . Sartre, in this work, has destroyed black zeal. . . . I needed to lose myself completely in negritude. . . . In any case, I *needed* not to know. "[40]

Has there ever been so eloquent a rage against the Medusan face of theory? Bhabha, at once joining forces with and recoiling from post-structuralism, asks, "How [are] we . . . to re-think 'ourselves' once we have undermined the immediacy and autonomy of self-consciousness"[41] (which is to say, once we have placed 'ourselves' between scare quotes)? This, he says, must be left as an open question.[42] Unfortunately, a politics founded upon open questions must founder upon these questions; such a politics turns out, once again, to be no politics at all.

What's apparent is that the shared subject of Gilroy and Mercer's exchange is, in fact, less black British cultural production than the role of the black British cultural critic. The conflict is not between two intellectuals; it is symptomatic of the impossible equilibrium that subtends all diasporic criticism. Yes, we can refuse populist modernism as a universal ethics, as a modality of privilege; no, we cannot dismiss it as inherently pernicious. If there's a Richard Wright in every minority critic, we have no better hope of making peace with him than he had of making peace with himself.

The Marionette Theater of the Political

The dilemmas of oppositional criticism haunt the fractured American critical community as well. The 1980s and 1990s witnessed not only a resurgence of what I'll call the "new moralism," but also the beginnings of its subsidence. And this development, too, was very much bound up with the problematic of representation, such that the relation between the politics of theory and the politics of politics became a question to be indefinitely deferred or finessed.

The hermeneutics of the 1970s killed the author; the politics of the 1980s brought the author back. As John Guillory pointed out quite perceptively in an essay on "the pedagogic imaginary," the debate over the canon entailed the resurrection of the author, this time as the representative of a social constituency.[43] The debate over canon formation was concerned, in the first instance, with *authors*, not with texts.

And as diasporic critics, we came to play a similar role, in a marionette theater of the political. The result was a certain amount of attendant acrimony. Edward Said early on noted this unsavory tendency, which he described as the "badgering, hectoring, authoritative tone" that persisted in contemporary Cultural Studies, adding, "The great horror I think we should all feel is toward systematic or dogmatic orthodoxies of one sort of another that are paraded as the last word of high Theory still hot from the press."[44] Is it merely the uncanny workings of William Wimsatt's imitative fallacy that accounts for the authoritarian modalities of scholarship, and scholarly intercourse, where issues of domination are foregrounded?

Again, I want to stress the way in which minority criticism can become a site for larger contestations. Robert Young, as an editor of the *Oxford Literary Review*, ventured an intriguing proposition in an essay entitled "The Politics of 'The Politics of Literary Theory.'" He notes that literary Marxism in contemporary America (as opposed to in Britain) has "few links with the social sciences or with a political base in the public sphere. You can make almost any political claims you like: you know that there is no danger that it will ever have any political effect." "At the same time," he continues, "the pressure of feminism, and more recently Black Studies, has meant that today the political cannot be ignored by anyone, and may be responsible for the white male retreat into Marxism. Marxism can compete with feminism and Black Studies insofar as it offers to return literary criticism to its traditional moral function, but can, more covertly, also act as a defence against them."[45] I just throw this out, but what this relation among Marxism and feminism and Black Studies points to is a struggle for the moral high ground.

And I think you could argue that this return to a gestural sort of politics, which still obtains in the bloody terrain of Cultural Studies, reflects a moralizing strain in contemporary criticism that has lost faith in its epistemological claims. If we can't tell you what's true and what's false, we'll at least tell you what's right and what's wrong. What's wrong? Racism, colonialism, class oppression, cultural imperialism, patriarchy, epistemic violence—the usual suspects. Anyway, we lost fact, and we got back ethics. A trade-in, but not necessarily an upgrade.

The New Moralism

I can give you a characteristic example of a now-familiar version of the politics of interpretation. I once read an unpublished paper by an extremely distinguished scholar that actually attacked Spike Lee for being responsible, though perhaps indirectly, for the death of black youths, echoing the well-known exchange between Phil Mushnick and Lee in *Sports Illustrated*, which actually resulted in a cover story entitled "Your Sneakers or Your Life." I'll explain the logic of the argument. Here's Spike, who sells Nikes—he directs and stars in commercials that promote Air Jordans, right?—and then here's the devastated, crack-ridden inner city, and then here's a dead black youth, bullet through the brain or maybe stabbed in the stomach, murdered for those Air Jordans. And all because Spike said that he's gotta have it. You think Mars Blackmon is funny? Those commercials have a body count.

I'm not exaggerating. This was a state-of-the-art critical essay,[46] which represents the impasse we've reached in the American academy. This is how we've been taught to do cultural politics. You find the body. Then you find the culprit. It's also where the critique of the commodity will lead you. It's an old phenomenon on the left (and certain kinds of Marxism can be very theological on this point): Commodification is like original sin, and any cultural form it touches is tainted. And yet these critiques are usually anchored to semi-organic notions of authenticity.

(Hazel Carby has criticized my valorization of urban vernacular forms, and beyond that the very concept of the vernacular, for being too easily appropriable, let's say, to this kind of perspective—and I think she has a point.)

The old leftist critiques of the commodity have a usefully confining tendency: The critiques set up a cunning trap that practically guarantees that the marginalized cultures being glorified will remain marginalized. The authors of these critiques knew just how to keep us in our place. And the logic was breathtakingly simple: If you win, you lose.

And that's because it's just a fact about the current conjuncture that if a cultural form reaches a substantial audience, it has entered the circuits of commodification. Gilroy explored this phenomenon with great subtlety in his Du Bois Lectures at Harvard in 2006, entitled "On the Moral Economy of Blackness."[47] Populist modernism stays in good ideological odor so long as it doesn't get too popular. And one of the most important contributions of the younger black British theorists has been a critique of the old critique of the commodity form. Mercer explores ways in which commodity forms have been expressively manipulated by the marginalized to explore and explode the artificiality of the identities to which they've been confined. (What's wrong with a conk? Mercer asks. Does it *have* to signify "racial" shame? Given the historic association of people of color with "nature," isn't it ironic to be insisting on the "naturalness" of their culture—not to mention hair?)

If Isaac Julien signs up for a distribution deal for one of his films, such as *Young Soul Rebels*, should we start hating him? Among proponents of the black British renascence, there's been a tendency to use a presumed polarity between Spike and Isaac to police the borders of black cultural production. Spike, corporate populism, Universal Studios: bad. Isaac, collectivist, independent cinema: good. You hear that in the American cineaste circuit. In Britain, you could get a different opposition set up. Isaac, high-falutin' Europeanized aesthetic, mostly white audience, darling of the highbrows: bad. *Ceddo*, nationalistic, naturalistic, dreadlocks, mostly black audience: good. Well, as Mr. Dooley says, you pays yer money and takes your pick.

I want to propose that it's worth distinguishing between morality and moralism. I want to propose that criticism doesn't always fulfill an ethico-political desideratum. But I do so with trepidation. As Logan Pearsall Smith has observed, "That we should practice what we preach is generally admitted; but anyone who preaches what he and his hearers practice must incur the gravest moral disapprobation."

A friend of mine suggested that we make official, that is, institutionalize, what we already do implicitly at conferences on "minority discourse": award a prize at the end for the panelist, respondent, or contestant most oppressed. Then at the end of the year, we could have the "Oppression Emmy Awards."[48] What became clear, by the end of 1990s, was that this establishment of what J. G. Melquior calls an "official marginality" meant that minority critics were accepted by the academy, but in return, they must accept a role already scripted for them. The rejected return triumphant. You think of Sally Field's address to the Motion Picture Academy when she received her Oscar. "You like me! You really, really like me!" we authorized others shriek into the microphone, exultation momentarily breaking our dour countenances. (We can, of course, be a little more self-conscious about it and acknowledge our problematic positionality: "You like me! You really, really like me—you racist, patriarchal, Eurotrash elitists!")

What moralism had to confront was the nature of commodified post-modern ethnicity—which we could describe as the Benetton's model. "All the colors of the world," none of the oppression. It was a seductive vision: cashmere instead of power relations.

And it *was* a change. Usually, the third world presented itself to us as the page people turn when the ad says you can help little Maria or you can turn the page. It was a tropological locale of suffering and destitution. Now little Maria's wearing a purple cashmere scarf and a black V-neck sweater, and the message is: You can have *style* like Maria here and shop at Benetton—or don't you give a damn about ethnic harmony?

The Benettonization of the first world was not without its ironies. In New York, as Patricia Williams has pointed out, they may not buzz you in if you actually look like one of those "ethnic" models.[49] Or, again, think of the controversy over the Benetton's ad that showed a black hand and a white hand cuffed together. Many people found it disturbing, because they assumed that the black was the prisoner. The image itself was perfectly symmetrical, which demonstrates how real-world power relations determine the way images are actually read.

Is academic politics finally a highbrow version of what *Women's Wear Daily* would call the "style wars"? I think that too easily lets us off the hook of history; it's the sort of newly fashionable cynicism that's based on an overly reductionist conception of the political. So even though I want to agree with Gayatri Spivak and others that criticism need not be, in the first instance, an "ethico-political" project—and that many of our critical debates have referents more immediate and mundane than their ostensible concerns—I also find something attractive in the Trotskyite vision of an historic bloc that wills itself out of existence when its purpose has been filled. Can global, imperializing theory *will* itself out of existence once its time has passed? Can we wave what Burke called the "fairy wand of philosophy," and say, "Vanish"?

In my next chapter, I want to trespass through what may be the last refuge of theory's imperial hope—the discursive locale of the third world itself. In that chapter, I'll be tracing, not the burden of Burke, but the phantom of Fanon.

CHAPTER THREE

Critical Fanonism

This book, it is hoped, will be a mirror.
FRANTZ FANON, *BLACK SKIN, WHITE MASKS*

O ne of the signal developments in contemporary criticism has been the ascendancy of the colonial paradigm. And to a marked degree, what has accompanied this turn is the reinstatement of Frantz Fanon as a global theorist. In 1996, Isaac Julien produced a remarkable film, *Frantz Fanon: Black Skin, White Masks*, featuring, incredibly, both Stuart Hall and Homi Bhabha, which implicitly assessed the role of Fanon's theories of culture, race, and nation in the history of Britain's vibrant Black Arts Movement and effectively canonized him as the patron saint of black British cultural studies. Robert Young canonized Fanon in the history of post-structuralism through a marvelously accessible overview of his work in the introduction to *Postcolonialism*, published in 2001, a year after David Macey had published his magisterial life of Fanon and two years after Nigel Gibson had collected a plethora of interpretations of Fanon's life and works from a multiplicity of critical and ideological approaches. Bhabha and Kwame Anthony Appiah have both published editions of *Black Skin, White Masks*, and Bhabha's "Foreword" to his edition of Fanon's *The Wretched of the Earth* masterfully points to Fanon as the proto-theorist of "the fin de siècle and the end of the cold war" through "a genealogy for globalization." Bhabha, writing in a 2004 world riven by tribalism, ethnic cleansing, fundamentalism, al-Qaeda, and Iraq, says that Fanon—who died of leukemia in 1961, just a year after Richard Wright had died, five years after both had met at the Amphithéâtre Descartes at the First International Conference of Negro Writers and Artists—is even useful for explaining this post–Berlin Wall, post–cold war world of ours: "I have tried, in this essay, to trace the prophecies of Fanon's living hand as it rises again to beckon enigmatically toward our own times." There is a Fanon for all seasons.[1]

Nor has the resurgence of interest in him been confined to those engaged in third world or subaltern studies. In a collection of essays centered on British Romanticism, Jerome McGann opens a discussion of William Blake and Ezra Pound with an extended invocation of Fanon. Donald Pease has used Fanon to open an attack on Stephen Greenblatt's reading of the Henriad and the interdisciplinary practices of the New Historicism. And Fanon—and published interpretations of Fanon—has even become regularly cited in the rereadings of the Renaissance that have emerged from places such as Sussex, Essex, and Birmingham.[2]

My intent is not to offer a reading of Fanon to supplant these others, but to read, even if summarily, some of these readings *of* Fanon. By focusing on successive appropriations of this figure, as both totem and text, I think we can chart out an itinerary through contemporary colonial discourse theory. I want to stress, then, that my ambitions here are extremely limited; what follows may be a prelude to a reading of Fanon, but does not even begin that task itself.[3]

Fanon's current fascination for us has something to do with a convergence of the problematic of colonialism with that of subject formation. As a psychoanalyst of culture, as a champion of the wretched of the earth, he is an almost irresistible figure for a criticism that sees itself as both oppositional and post-modern.

And yet there's something *Rashomon*-like about his contemporary guises. It may be a matter of judgment whether his writings are riven with contradiction or richly dialectical, polyvocal, and multivalent. They are in any event highly porous to interpretation, and the readings they elicit are, as a result, of unfailing *symptomatic* interest: Frantz Fanon, not to put too fine a point on it, is a Rorschach inkblot with legs.

We might begin with an essay by Edward Said entitled "Representing the Colonized." To Jean-François Lyotard's vision of the decline of grand narrative, Said counterposes the counter-narratives of liberation that Fanon (as he says) "forces on a Europe playing 'le jeu irresponsible de la belle au bois dormant.'"[4] And Said goes on to argue:

> Despite its bitterness and violence, the whole point of Fanon's work is to force the European metropolis to think its history *together with* the history of colonies awakening from the cruel stupor and

abused immobility of imperial domination. . . . Alone, and without due recognition allowed for the colonial experience, Fanon says, the Western narratives of enlightenment and emancipation are revealed as so much windy hypocrisy. . . .

I do not think that the anti-imperialist challenge represented by Fanon and Cesaire or others like them has by any means been met; neither have we taken them seriously as models or representations of human effort in the contemporary world. In fact, Fanon and Cesaire—of course I speak of them as types—jab directly at the question of identity and of identitarian thought, that secret sharer of present anthropological reflection on "otherness" and "difference." What Fanon and Cesaire required of their own partisans, even during the heat of struggle, was to abandon fixed ideas of settled identity and culturally authorized definition. Become different, they said, in order that your fate as colonized peoples can *be* different.[5]

I've given some space to these remarks because it is, preeminently, in passages such as this one that Fanon as global theorist has been produced.

And yet some have found cause for objection here. Reading the passage from Said, they say that given the grand narrative in which Fanon is himself inserted, it seems beside the point to ask about the extent to which the historical Fanon really did abandon all fixity of identity; beside the point to raise questions about his perhaps ambivalent relation to counter-narratives of identity; beside the point to address his growing political and philosophical estrangement from Césaire. Fanon's individual specificity seems beside the point because what we have here is explicitly a composite figure, indeed, an ethnographic construct. It's made clear by the formulaic reference to Fanon, Césaire, and "others like them." It's made clear when Said writes, "Of course I speak of them as types"—to which some readers will pose the question, "Why 'of course'?" And they will answer, "Because the ethnographer always speaks of his subjects as types." Or they find the answer in Albert Memmi, who explains that a usual "sign of the colonized's depersonalization is what we might call the mark of the plural. The colonized is never characterized in an individual manner; he is entitled only to drown in an anonymous collectivity."[6]

Thus, while calling for a recognition of the *situatedness* of all discourses, the critic delivers a Fanon as a global theorist *in vacuo*. In the course of an appeal for the specificity of the other, we discover that this

global theorist of alterity is emptied of his own specificity. In the course of a critique of identitarian
thought, Fanon is conflated with someone who proved
in important respects an ideological antagonist. And
so on.

These moves are, I think, all too predictable and,
yes, even beside the point. Said has delivered a brief
for a usable culture; it is not to be held against him
that his interest is in mobilizing a usable Fanon. Indeed, this is his own counter-narrative, in the terrain
of post-colonial criticism. But Said's use of Fanon to
allegorize the site of counter-hegemonic agency must
also be read as an implicit rejoinder to those who have
charged him with ignoring the colonized's own self-
representations; Homi Bhabha's objection that Said's
vision of Orientalism suggests that "power and discourse is possessed entirely by the colonizer" is typical
in this regard.[7]

Certainly, Bhabha's own readings of Fanon during the
last twenty-five years are the most elaborated that
have been produced in the field of post-structuralism.
And his readings are designed to breach the disjunction Said's essay may appear to preserve: between the

discourse of the colonized and that of the colonizer. And among Bhabha's several essays on Fanon, I want to take some time to consider his seminal essay, "Remembering Fanon: Self, Psyche, and the Colonial Condition," because of its exemplary insights into the complexities of Fanon's thinking about culture, discourse, and colonialism—insights that, in turn, rightfully generated a huge amount of interest in Fanon among all sorts of cultural critics after the essay's publication in 1986—and because this work is symptomatic of a larger phenomenon that I am attempting to trace in this chapter.[8]

For Bhabha, colonial ambivalence "makes the boundaries of colonial positionality—the division of self-other—and the question of colonial power—the differentiation of colonizer/colonized—different from both the master-slave dialectic or the phenomenological projection of 'otherness.'"[9] Accordingly, he has directed attention to (what he sees as) the disruptive articulations of the colonized as inscribed in colonial discourse, that is, the discourse of the colonized.

Bhabha's reading requires a model of self-division, of "alienation within identity," and he has enlisted Lacanian psychoanalysis to this end. "[Minority discourse] is not simply the attempt to invert the balance of power within an unchanged order of discourse, but to redefine the symbolic process through which the social Imaginary—Nation, Culture, or Community—become 'subjects' of discourse and 'objects' of psychic identification."[10] From Fanon, Bhabha educes the question, How can a human being live otherwise? And Bhabha juxtaposes to his reflections on *Black Skin, White Masks* the following remarks of Jacques Lacan's: "In the case of display, . . . the play of combat in the form of intimidation, the being gives of himself, or receives from the other, something that is like a mask, a double, an envelope, a thrown-off skin, thrown off in order to cover the frame of shield. It is through this separated form of himself that the being comes into play in his effects of life and death."[11]

Bhabha may be Fanon's closest reader, and it is an oddly touching performance of a coaxing devotion. He regrets aloud those moments in Fanon that cannot be reconciled to the post-structuralist critique of identity, because he wants Fanon to be even better than he is. Benita Parry has described Bhabha as proffering Fanon as "a premature poststructuralist," and I don't think Bhabha would disagree.[12]

In this same vein, Bhabha redescribes Fanon's "Manichean delirium" as a condition internalized within colonial discourse, as a form of self-misrecognition.

"In articulating the problem of colonial cultural alienation in the psychoanalytic language of demand and desire, Fanon radically questions the formation of both individual and social authority as they come to be developed in the discourse of social sovereignty."[13] Fanon's representation "turns on the idea of Man as his alienated image, not Self and Other but the 'Otherness' of the Self inscribed in the perverse palimpsest of colonial identity."[14] It's interesting to note, however, that Bhabha's mobilization of Lacan stands as an explicit correction of Fanon's own citation of Lacan in *Black Skin, White Masks*.

Here, then, is the moment that might be seen as the originary irruption of Lacan into colonial discourse theory. With reference to the mirror stage, Fanon writes: "When one has grasped the mechanism described by Lacan, one can have no further doubt that the real Other for the white man is and will continue to be the black man. And conversely. Only for the white man, the Other is perceived on the level of the body image, absolutely the not-self, that is, the unidentifiable, the unassimilable. For the black man, historical and economic realities come into the picture."[15] (Hence for the delirious Antillean, Fanon tells us, "the mirror hallucination is always neutral. When Antilleans tell me that they have experienced it, I al-

ways ask the same question: 'What color were you?'
Invariably they reply: 'I had no color.'")[16]

Bhabha cautions, however, that "the place of the
Other must not be imaged as Fanon sometimes suggests as a fixed phenomenological point, opposed to
the Self, that represents a culturally alien consciousness.
The Other must be seen as the necessary negation of
a primordial identity—cultural and psychic—that in-
troduces the system of differentiation which enables
the 'cultural' to be signified as a linguistic, symbolic,
historical reality."[17] In other words, Bhabha wants
Fanon to mean Lacan rather than, say, Sartre, but ac-
knowledges that Fanon does tend to slip. "At times
Fanon . . . turns too hastily from the ambivalences of
identification to the antagonistic identities of political
alienation and cultural discrimination; he is too quick
to name the Other, to personalize its presence in the
language of colonial racism. . . . These attempts . . .
can at time, blunt the edge of Fanon's brilliant illus-
trations of the complexity of psychic projections in
the pathological colonial relation."[18]

Bhabha is charmingly up front about the pulling
and pushing involved in turning Fanon into *le Lacan
noir*. He regrets the moments when Fanon turns to
"an existential humanism that is as banal as it is be-
atific."[19] Indeed, Bhabha's rather passionate essay,

entitled "Remembering Fanon," can as easily be read as an index to all that Bhabha wants us to forget.

For some oppositional critics, however, the hazards of Bhabha's approach may go beyond interpretive etiquette. Thus, in a prelude to his own Lacanian reading of colonial discourse, Abdul JanMohamed takes Bhabha to task for downplaying the negativity of the colonial encounter, and not surprisingly, his critique pivots on his own positioning of Fanon. JanMohamed writes, "Though he cites Frantz Fanon, Bhabha completely ignores Fanon's definition of the conqueror/native relation as a 'Manichean" struggle—a definition that is not a fanciful metaphoric caricature but an accurate representation of a profound conflict." "What does it mean, in practice, to imply as Bhabha does that the native, whose entire economy and culture are destroyed, is somehow in 'possession' of colonial power?" he asks. JanMohamed charges that Bhabha asserts "the unity of the 'colonial subject'" and so "represses the political history of colonialism."[20]

The critical double bind these charges raise is clear enough. You can discursively empower the native and open yourself to charges of downplaying the epistemic (and literal) violence of colonialism, or you can play up the absolute nature of colonial domination and be open to charges of negating the subjectivity and agency of the colonized, thus textually replicating the repressive operations of colonialism. In agency, so it seems, begins responsibility.

But, of course, JanMohamed does not argue that colonialism completely destroyed the native's culture. Conversely, it can't be the case that Bhabha ignores Fanon's discussion of colonialism's self-representation as a Manichean world, because he explicitly reflects on what Fanon calls the "Manichean delirium." But Bhabha certainly does offer a different account of it—an account that makes it unlikely that he is positing a unity of the colonial subject in the way JanMohamed construes it, for Bhabha's account denies the unity of either subject in the first place. Properly reframed, JanMohamed's argument might be seen as another version of a critique of Lacan advanced by (among others) Stephen Heath, who argues that "the importance of this idea of the Other [as the "locus" of the symbolic, which produces the subject as constitutively divided] and the symbolic is crucial in Lacan exactly because it allows him to abstract from problems of social-historical determinations."[21] As against Fredric Jameson's famous injunction, then, Lacan's motto would turn out to be "Never historicize; never explain."

But far from turning against the psychoanalytic model of colonial discourse, JanMohamed's concern is, of course, to advance an explicitly Lacanian account of these discourses. To be sure, the allure of Lacan for both Bhabha and JanMohamed is only tangentially related to its appearance in Fanon. As I've suggested, Lacan's is exemplarily a discourse that maps a problematic of subject formation onto a self-other model that seems to lend itself to the colonial encounter. On the other hand, it's unclear whether JanMohamed really wants to make space for all the distinctively Lacanian ramifications that we heard Bhabha spell out.

For his part, JanMohamed reinstates the notions of alterity that Bhabha has rejected. "Faced with an incomprehensible and multifaceted alterity," he writes, "the European theoretically has the option of responding to the Other in terms of identity or difference."[22] Here, the other exists as such, prior to and independent of the encounter. But a little further on we find the limits of the Lacanian register in Jan-Mohamed's analysis: "Genuine and thorough comprehension of Otherness," he writes, requires "the virtually impossible task of negating one's very being."[23] This "virtually impossible" encounter is neither a provisional, negotiated difference, nor is it the Lacanian other in whose field the self must constitute itself. Rather, it is a close encounter of the third kind, involving the disputed notion of radical alterity.[24]

And the binarity supports his division of colonialist literature into the two categories of the imaginary and the symbolic. In the imaginary text, the native functions as mirror, though in fact negative, image. The symbolic text uses the native as mediator of European desires, introducing a realm of "intersubjectivity, heterogeneity, and particularity" as opposed to the infantile specularity of otherness that the imaginary text enacts.

Although this use of Lacan to demarcate literary categories (an application that has been criticized as crudely empiricist) has uncertain value as a means of classifying colonial literature, it has appeal in classifying post-colonial theorists. Here we might station JanMohamed's penchant for Manichean allegories in the imaginary register, Bhabha's negotiations in the symbolic. I suppose (to continue the conceit) we might cast Fanon as the other that mediates between them and the historical real.

But what has proven most problematic in JanMohamed's theorizing is what critics describe as an overly mimeticist conception of oppositional literature.

Here we should turn to an overview of colonial discourse theory by radical South African expatriate Benita Parry. In the course of an explicitly Fanonian critique, Parry tasks JanMohamed's study for lacking "Fanon's grasp of the paradoxes and pitfalls of 'rediscovering tradition' and representing it within a western system of meanings. What for Fanon is a transitional process of liberating the consciousness of the oppressed into a new reality, JanMohamed treats as the arrival of the definitive oppositional discourse."[25]

In fact, the critique of alterity as pursued in Gayatri Spivak and Bhabha concerns her even more. Parry asks, "What are the politics of projects which dissolve the binary opposition colonial self/colonized other, encoded in colonialist language as a dichotomy necessary to domination, but also differently inscribed in the discourse of liberation as a dialectic of conflict and a call to arms?"[26] Thus, Parry says of Bhabha's reading that it "obscures Fanon's paradigm of the colonial condition as one of implacable enmity between native and invader, making armed opposition both a cathartic and pragmatic necessity."[27] (To be sure, Fanon also spoke of the metaphysics of the dualism as "often quite fluid.")[28]

Of both Spivak and Bhabha, Parry asserts, "Because their theses admit of no point outside of discourse from which opposition can be engendered their project is concerned to place incendiary devices within the dominant structures of representation and not to confront these with knowledge."[29] Considering the subaltern voice to be irretrievable, they devalue the actual counter-narratives of anti-colonialist struggle as mere reverse discourse. But what Fanon shows us, according to Parry, and what "colonial discourse theory has not taken on board," is that "a cartography of imperialist ideology more extensive than its address in the colonialist space, as well as a conception of the native as historical subject and agent of an oppositional discourse is needed."[30]

To such positions in contemporary theory, Parry contrasts what she implies is a more properly Fanonian critical mode, one that would

> also reject totalizing abstractions of power as falsifying situations of domination and subordination, [and in which] the notion of hegemony is inseparable from that of a counter-hegemony. In this theory of power and context, the process of procuring the consent of the oppressed and the marginalized to the existing structure of relationships through ideological inducements, necessarily generates dissent and resistance, since the subject

is conceived as being constituted by means of incommensurable solicitations and heterogeneous social practices. The outcome of this agonistic exchange, in which those addressed challenge their interlocutors, is that the hegemonic discourse is ultimately abandoned as scorched earth when a different discourse, forged in the process of disobedience and combat, occupying new, never colonized and "utopian" territory, and prefiguring other relationships, values, and aspirations, is enunciated.[31]

Some people might describe this utopian moment as the externalization of the quest romance. But note the emergence here of the familiar historicist dialectic of subversion and containment: That power produces its own subversion is held to be a fact about the constitution of the subject itself. And some will be skeptical about the notion of a revolutionary literature that is implicit here. If Said made of Fanon an advocative of post-post-modern counter-narratives of liberation, if JanMohamed made of Fanon a Manichean theorist of colonialism as absolute negation, and if Bhabha cloned, from Fanon's *theoria*, another third world post-structuralist, Parry's Fanon (which I generally find persuasive) turns out to confirm her own rather optimistic vision of literature and social action. "This book, it is hoped, will be a mirror," wrote a twenty-six-year-old Fanon, and in rereading these readings, including Bhabha's own recent revisioning of Fanon as prophet of our post–cold war post–9/11 world order, I find it hard to avoid a sort of tableau of narcissism, with Fanon himself as the other that can only reflect and consolidate the critical self.

And perhaps we can hear a warning about the too uncritical appropriations of a Fanon in Spivak's famous rebuttal to the criticism concerning the recuperation or effacement of the native's voice. The course we've been plotting leads us, then, to what is, in part, Spivak's critique of Benita Parry's critique of Abdul JanMohamed's critique of Homi Bhabha's critique of Edward Said's critique of colonial discourse.

Now, in Spivak's view, Parry "is in effect bringing back the 'native informant syndrome' and using it differently in a critique of neo-colonialism."[32] When Benita Parry takes us—and by this I mean Homi Bhabha, Abdul JanMohamed, Gayatri Spivak—to task for not being able to listen to the natives or to let the natives speak, she forgets that we are natives, too. We talk like Defoe's Friday, only much better.[33] Thus, in straining for a voice of indigenous resistance, we can succumb to another quest romance, this time for the transparent "real" voice of the native. This has so many of the properties of a somewhat displaced model in the 19th century class stratified management of the culture of imperialism, that I believe that it is my task now to be vigilant about this desire to hear the native. Also, let me tell you that the native's not a fool and within the fact of this extraordinary search for the "true" native which has been going on for decades, perhaps even a century or more, the native himself or herself is aware of this particular value.[34]

So we need to reject, says Spivak, that insidious image of the native as a para-human creature "who is there to give us evidence that we must always trust (as we wouldn't trust the speech of people to whom we ascribe the complexity of being human)."[35]

I think this is an elegant reminder and safeguard against the sentimental romance of alterity. On the other hand, it still leaves space for some versions of Parry's critique. I suggest that we try to distinguish more sharply between the notions of cultural resistance, on the one hand, and of cultural alterity, on the other, even as we note the significance of their conflation. There may well be something familiar about Spivak's insistence on the totalizing embrace of colonial discourse and Parry's unease with the insistence.

My claim is that what Jacques Derrida calls writing, Spivak, in a brilliant reversal, has renamed colonial discourse. So it is no accident that the two terms share precisely the same functionality. The Derridian *mot*, that there is nothing outside the text, is reprised as the argument that there is nothing outside (the discourse of) colonialism. And it leads, as well, to the argument that this very discourse must be read as heterogeneous to itself, as laced with the aporias and disjunctures that any deconstructive reading must elicit and engage. (It's in just these terms that Spivak joins in the critique of alterity: "I am critical of the binary opposition colonizer/colonized. I try to examine the heterogeneity of 'colonial power' and to disclose the complicity of the two poles of that opposition as it constitutes the disciplinary enclave of the critique of imperialism.")[36] Indeed, I think Spivak's argument, put in its strongest form, entails the corollary that all discourse is colonial discourse.

———

But perhaps the psychoanalytic model of culture makes this a foregone conclusion. When Fanon asserted that "only a psychoanalytical interpretation of the black problem" could explain "the structure of the complex,"[37] he was perhaps only extending a line of Sigmund Freud's, which Stephen Greenblatt has brought attention to: "Civilization behaves toward sexuality as a people or a stratum of its population does which has subjected another one to its exploitation."[38] Freud's pessimistic vision of "analysis interminable" would then refer us to a process of decolonization interminable.

I spoke of this double session of paradigms in which the Freudian mechanisms of psychic repression are set in relation to those of colonial repression. But it's still unclear whether we are to speak of convergence or mere parallelism. Again, the Fanonian text casts the problem in sharpest relief.

Stephan Feuchtwang has cogently argued, in an essay entitled "Fanonian Spaces," that

the use of psychoanalytic categories for descriptions of social situations has tremendous analogical virtues. One is their capacity to indicate a directionality of affect in the situations, of forces mobilized rather than a mere disposition of intelligible elements and their rationality. Another is their focus on the relational, truly the social facts. Fanon

does not analyze the colonial situation as a con-
tract of cultural subjects or as an interaction of
interested subjects as if they were logically prior
to the situation. Instead, the relations of the situation are analyzed to see how their organization
forms cultural subjects."[39]

Feuchtwang speaks of "tremendous analogical
virtues," but are they *merely* analogical? Furthermore—
accepting the force of the Freudian rereading—do
we really want to elide the distance between political
repression and individual neurosis: the *positional* distance between Steve Biko and, say, Woody Allen? On
the other hand, Feuchtwang does point to the problematic relation between individual case studies and
analyses of the collective state in *Black Skin, White
Masks*. We've heard Fanon speak of the necessity for
the "psychoanalytic interpretation," yet he subse-
quently juxtaposes a notion of socioanalysis to Freud's
psychoanalysis: "It will be seen that the black man's
alienation is not an individual question. Besides [the
Freudian contribution of] phylogeny and ontogeny
stands sociogeny."[40]

Or as Albert Memmi simplifies the question, in
the preface to his classic *The Colonizer and the Colonized*: "Does psychoanalysis win out over Marxism?

Does all depend on the individual or on society?"[41] And, of course, the tension—which we endlessly try to theorize away—persists in all political appropriations of psychoanalysis.

Indeed, doesn't it plague our appropriation of Fanon as a collectivized individual, as alterity in revolt, as the third world of theory itself? I speak, of course, of *our* Fanon, of whom Sartre wrote in the preface of *The Wretched of the Earth*, "The Third World finds *itself* and speaks to *itself* in his voice."[42] I speak of the black Benjamin who, as Jerome McGann writes, presents "the point of view of a Third World, where the dialectic of the first two worlds is completely reimagined," because he writes from "the perspective of an actual citizen of the actual Third World."[43]

So I want to turn, finally, to yet another Fanon, the ironic figure analyzed by Tunisian novelist and philosopher Albert Memmi. Memmi's Fanon is, emphatically, not the Fanon we have recuperated for global colonial discourse theory. He is, indeed, a far more harried subject, a central fact of whose life was his dislocation from the "actual Third World." Of course, we know from his biographers and from his own account that Fanon, whose mother was of Alsatian descent, grew up in Martinique thinking of himself as white and French and that his painful reconstitution as a black West Indian occurred only when he arrived at the French capital. Yet at this point—again, in Memmi's narrative—Fanon lost himself as a black Martinican: "Fanon's private drama is that, though henceforth hating France and the French, he will never turn to Négritude and to the West Indies"; indeed, he "never again set foot in Martinique."[44] Homi Bhabha, summarizing this line of Memmi's thinking about this curious phenomenon, argues that "Fanon's commitment to the Algerian cause seemed to turn from a political commitment into a more inward identification, a consummate self-fashioning of himself as an Algerian," manifesting itself in "a compensatory family romance that would disavow his Martinican origins."[45] Yet Fanon's attempts to identify himself as an Algerian proved equally doomed. As Fanon's biographers remind us, most Algerian revolutionaries scant his role and remain irritated by the attention paid to him in the West as a figure in Algerian decolonization. To them—and how ironic this is to his Western admirers—he remained a European interloper. In Tunisia, Bhabha reports, he was once known as "the pamphleteer from Martinique."[46]

Though Fanon worked as a psychiatrist in Algeria and Tunisia, in neither country did he even understand the language; his psychiatric consultations were conducted through an interpreter.[47] And the image here—of the psychoanalysis of culture being conducted, quite literally, through an *interpreter*—does speak eloquently of the ultimately mediated nature of the most anti-colonialist analysis.

Far from championing the particularities and counter-narratives of the oppressed, Memmi's Fanon is an interloper without the patience or interest to acquaint himself with the local specificities of culture: "He grew impatient and failed to hide his scorn of regional particularisms, the tenacity of traditions and customs that distinguish cultural and national aspirations, not to speak of contradictory interests."[48] And although Memmi's own insertion in colonial politics is certainly complex, his version is consistent with that of the revolutionary elite of post-independent Algeria.

Memmi's Fanon was devoted to a dream of a third world, a third world where he could look into a mirror and have no color. Yet he lived in a third world that rebuffed his most ardent desires for identification. What remained for him, Memmi writes, "but to propose a completely novel man?"[49]

We've seen suggested, at various points, the disruptive relation between narratives of subject formation and narratives of liberation inscribed on the Fanonian text (as well as in contemporary colonial discourse theory more widely). Memmi is quite blunt on the issue: Fanon does, on the one hand, claim an absolute disjunction between colonial representations of the colonized and the subject of representation. But, Memmi writes, doesn't colonialism inscribe itself upon the colonized? "For that matter, is Fanon's own thinking on this point really coherent? I too could cite a great many contradictory passages of his, where he speaks of 'mutilation,' 'inferiorization,' 'criminal impulsion,'—results, obviously, of colonization."[50] Actually, Memmi goes on to say, Fanon must have seen that the personality of the colonized was affected in these ways. But "he found them embarrassing and repulsive. This is because, like many other defenders of the colonized, he harbored a certain amount of revolutionary romanticism. . . . As for most social romantics, so for him the victim remained proud and intact throughout oppression; he suffered but did not let himself be broken. And the day oppression ceases, the new man is supposed to appear before our eyes immediately." But, says Memmi, "this is not the way it happens."[51]

I believe that the Antillean mirror that reflects no color at all haunts Fanon. Memmi is surely right to locate the utopian moment in Fanon in his depiction of decolonization as engendering "a kind of tabula rasa," as "quite simply the replacing of a certain 'species of men by another 'species' of men," so that the fear that we will continue to be (as he puts it) "overdetermined from without" was never reconciled with his political vision of emancipation.[52] This may be the clearest way of representing Fanon's own self-divisions, that is, as an agon between psychology and a politics, between ontogeny and sociogeny, between—to recur to Memmi—Marx and Freud.

Fanon's vision of the new man emerges as central tableau in identity politics, for us as for him. At the intersection of colonial and psychoanalytic discourse, Fanon wonders how to create a new identity. The problem remains, again for us as for him, that—as Memmi remarks about Fanon's own project of personal transformation—"one doesn't leave one's own self behind as easily as all that."[53]

———

Rehistoricizing Fanon, we can hear a lament concerning the limits of liberation, concerning the very intelligibility of his dream of decolonization. And even though the colonial paradigm proved valuable in foregrounding issues of power and positionality, now may be the time to question its ascendance in literary and cultural studies, especially because the "disciplinary enclave" of anti-imperialist discourse has proved a last bastion for the project, and dream, of global theory. In the context of the colonial binarism, we've seldom admitted fully how disruptive the psycho-analytic model can be, elaborating a productive rela-tion between oppressed and oppressor—productive of each as speaking subjects. And yet we can chart the torsional relation of the discourses in the exceptional instability of Fanon's own rhetoric.

But this requires of us that we no longer allow Fanon to remain a kind of icon or "screen memory," rehearsing dimly remembered dreams of post-colonial emancipation. It means *reading* him, with an acknowl-edgment of his own historical particularity, as an actor whose own search for self-transcendence scarcely ex-empted him from the heterogeneous and conflictual structures that we have taken to be characteristic of colonial discourse. It means not elevating him above his localities of discourse as a trans-cultural, trans-historical global theorist, not simply to cast him into battle, but to recognize him as a battlefield in himself. Fanon wrote, with uncanny and prescient insistence: "In no fashion should I undertake to prepare the world that will come later. I belong irreducibly to my time."[54]

Do we still need global, imperial theory, even the whole universalizing model of capital-T theory that it presupposes? It's no scandal that our own theoretical reflections must be as provisional, reactive, and local as the texts we reflect upon. Of course, discarding the imperial agenda of global theory also means not having to choose *between* or *among* Wright and Léopold Sédar Senghor; Césaire and Senghor; Spivak and Said; Greenblatt, Pease, and Porter; Bhabha and JanMohamed; Parry and Fredric Jameson and Aijaz Ahmad; or even Fanon and Memmi. Rather, it means not representing the choice as one of epistemic hygiene. And it requires a recognition that we, too, just as much as Fanon, may be fated to rehearse the agonisms of a culture that may never earn the title of *post*-colonial.[55]

CHAPTER FOUR

Beyond the Culture Wars: Identities in Dialogue

The Culture Wars: The Sequel

For literary and cultural critics, "the culture wars" were battles that raged during the late 1980s and 1990s, first and foremost, over which authors and which of their texts would be a part of the literary canon, the "classical," "timeless," or "universal" texts that we teach in survey courses, say, in American literature, or in "Great Books" courses, the texts that stand the test of time, the texts that—in some magical way—speak to the universal human condition. That battleground soon expanded to include heated confrontations over the rise of ethnic and gender studies programs (African American studies, women's studies, gay studies, etc.) and their proper place in any serious Faculty of Arts and Sciences, if, indeed, they should have any place at all as freestanding or even quasi-independent, tenure-granting entities. Who should get tenure and who decides who should get tenure became just as important, if not more so, than what courses tenured professors should be allowed to teach. I don't think that I am being too optimistic or naïve if I say, twenty years later, that these questions of pedagogy and appointments and promotion, are, in most parts of the academy, more or less resolved, with accounts of the culture wars being the stuff of undergraduate essays in English departments and Ph.D. theses in the humanities. After all, we won those wars, didn't we? Isn't Zora Neale Hurston taught just about everywhere these days?

Well, most certainly, in one significant sense, the opposition (that would be us) won the culture wars. After all, what self-respecting English department does not teach African American or women's literature? And ample Norton anthologies make the teaching of those traditions easy and, well, canonical, even one called *The Norton Anthology of Literature by Women,* and another called *The Norton Anthology of African American Literature,* best-sellers both. But I am beginning to believe that, even though we seem to have won these battles over the classroom, perhaps they were just fronts in a much larger, vaster, and more complicated campaign than most of us could possibly have grasped two decades ago.

Will the culture wars turn out to be our generation's twenty-first-century version of the seventeenth century's Thirty Years War? Are we to believe that the symbolic trade-off for the canonization of, say, *Their Eyes Were Watching God,* was the unending bitterness and enduring recalcitrance of the Red states? Could those battles in literature departments in the early 1990s possibly have contributed to the creation of "something new in our political life," as Michael Tomasky puts it, "the summer's apoplectic and bordering-on-violent town-hall meetings, and the large '9/12' rally on Washington's National mall that drew tens of thousands of people to protest America's descent into 'socialism' (or 'communism,' or, occasionally, 'Nazism')," replete with placards depicting President Barack Obama either as a Sambo-like version of Heath Ledger's The Joker or as Adolf Hitler in blackface? Was there any relation between what we achieved in the academy in terms of diversifying the canon and the "Tea Party" movement organized two decades later by FreedomWorks and a coalition of almost thirty other conservative organizations?[1] Even though the left won those heated battles fairly easily (in retrospect) against an aging and ill-prepared opposition within the cloistered confines of a traditionally liberal and tolerant academy, is it possible, even with all that the election of a liberal black president implies, that we could still lose the larger war with the right over core values of liberal democracy within American society?

Adam Gopnik, with unusually clear foresight as the canon wars raged around us, warned of this some fifteen years ago: "The left's ambitions are political and its triumphs cultural," he noted, "while the right's ambitions are cultural and its triumphs political."[2] Perhaps because of our own success with canon reformation within the university, for a long time I would find myself startled, even amused, by the use of the phrase "culture wars" in the popular press to refer to a melee that seemed to be explicitly political and only indirectly cultural, but most certainly not "cultural" in the sense of the English department and the canon of American literature. In a recent column, for example, Frank Rich wrote that "Americans have less and less patience for the intrusive and divisive moral scolds who thrived in the bubbles of the Clinton and Bush years. Culture wars are a luxury the country—the G.O.P. included—can no longer afford."[3] It is clear that the canon was nowhere on Frank Rich's mind. And if you do even a cursory search of the Internet for "culture wars," as I just did, it is clear that few people even remember the canon wars when they use the term. Of 1 million results for "culture wars," 217,000 referred to "abortion," 182,000 related to "evolution," 139,000 pointed to "immigration," 103,000 were concerned with "gay marriage," and almost 333,000 were about "Obama." Multiculturalism? 44,800 results. It is clear that what many of us among the professoriate thought was the war was merely a battle, a skirmish—an important one, certainly, but judging from the ferocity of the anger being vented, symbolically, upon President Obama's proposals for health care reform, for example, a skirmish nonetheless.

Although the "culture wars" in the early 1990s was an umbrella term that gathered under one rubric the flare-ups over abortion rights, gay rights, the use of federal funds to display Robert Mapplethorpe's nude images of black male bodies, feminism, affirmative action, Vice President Dan Quayle's "Murphy Brown" speeches, and the road show featuring Stanley Fish and Dinesh D'Souza, among other things, the conflict was always, in retrospect, burbling outside of academia, too. That's why even when the right was winning all the major battles—after all, George H. W. Bush's presidency was effectively the third term of Reaganism—people on the right remained crazily embittered. The ideological turn in the academy that I've been mentioning was something they latched onto, but their anger was part of a general sense that there was a broader substrate of social change that they were powerless to affect. The ire that we generated by what we were attempting to do in the classroom, especially protecting the diversity to which the best affirmative action programs aspire, was symptomatic of a phenomenon much, much larger, one that we see, at this writing, manifesting itself in an unprecedented degree of naked, financed, systematically organized, and sometimes quasi-racist venom directed at the nation's first black president.

But because the culture wars as these pertain to the study of culture and the canon provided the salient context and backdrop for the growth and appropriation of Cultural Studies in the United States, for the Black Arts Movement in Britain, and for the reappropriation of the critical writings of Frantz

Fanon as a central theorist of post-colonialism, I would like to attempt a sort of genealogy of those thrilling days of yesteryear before proffering my own brief for cultural pluralism, lest this curious history be forgotten, or its importance to the theoretical terrain that I am exploring in this book be underappreciated. And the *locus classicus* of that war would, without a doubt, be a speech delivered by a Republican presidential candidate in the summer of 1992.

The Culture Wars: The Prequel

"There is a religious war going on in this country for the soul of America. It is a cultural war, as critical to the kind of nation we shall be as the Cold War itself, for this war is for the soul of America." These words, you may recall, were spoken by Pat Buchanan at the 1992 Republican National Convention. (Some people were disturbed by his remarks, I know; one commentator did suggest they probably sounded better in the original German.)

As Buchanan had explained earlier that year, an adversarial and libertine culture was jeopardizing the very integrity of the republic. "As America's imperial troops guard frontiers all over the world," he said, "our own frontiers are open, and the barbarian is inside the gates. And you do not deal with the Vandals and the Visigoths who are pillaging your cities by expanding the Head Start and food stamp programs."[4]

You cannot buy off cultural combatants—we might charitably read this passage as saying—with material concessions. Those who rioted in response to Rodney King's beating by the police in Los Angeles, Buchanan told us, were merely enacting a script prepared for them by these same combatants of the cultural left.

Yes, 1992 was a summer of discontent for those who believed that the so-called culture wars had subsided into an uneasy civility, or were soon to do so. Attempting to engineer the rehabilitation of Vice President Quayle, his chief of staff, William Kristol, introduced into common parlance the term "cultural elite," evidently an adaptation of the term "new class" that intellectuals such as Midge Decter and Irving Kristol had tried to popularize in the mid-1970s. If it was less than clear exactly who was designated by the term "cultural elite," Vice President Quayle himself declared that he "wore their scorn as a badge of honor." He did not specify whether he wore everyone else's scorn as a badge of honor, too, or if he wore it in some other way, or if scorning the vice president automatically earned you a position in the cultural elite, in which case approximately 85 percent of Americans who were surveyed would have qualified for this selfsame elite. It was also left unclear whether criterion for membership in the elite was attitudinal or positional or some combination of the two.

But one thing we were assured was that this elite had contempt for the values of the ordinary American—possibly exempting the 85 percent of Americans who reportedly agreed at the time with a poor estimation of the vice president, an estimation worn as the aforementioned badge of honor. And possibly exempting, too, the teeming masses of Americans who watched their television shows and read their magazines with an avidity that guaranteed maximal advertising revenues. For the cultural elite, as it turned out in subsequent discussion, actually designated the capitalists of mass culture—that is to say, people who secured their position, much like our elected officials, by maintaining a competitive audience share. (What the derogation of the cultural elite—an enantiomer of the left and liberal admonitions concerning the corporate elite—reminds us is that for our electoral conservatives, enthusiasm for the free market does not extend to the free market in culture.) The salient difference between Quayle and his network counterparts was, of course, that Quayle wasn't canceled midway into his first season. A four-year run was guaranteed—even if the speeches were mostly reruns.

Politicizing "Politics"

But why dwell on the inanities of cultural warfare in popular political discourse in the early 1990s? I suppose because if you're interested in the history of the role assigned culture—so called—in the American political arena today, it's an obvious place to pause and consider. On another occasion, and in another context, I remarked that those who were with great anguish wringing their hands over an allegedly "politicized" academy were missing the irony of the outcome: the creation of a politics that was, in the worst sense, merely academic.

Let me elaborate on this. What do critics have in mind when they speak of a politicized curriculum? In part, they have in mind the explicit claim that the curriculum *is* political. Now, I won't bore you with a recitation of the doxa that there is no pristine and Archimedean space exempt from the political; by now we all know this by heart, and so long as politics is defined in an inclusive enough sense, I'm sure this is true enough. But that copula "is," is a fabulous labor-saving device. Pronouncing that the curriculum is political saves you from having to investigate and then to specify precisely *how* it comes to have political efforts or functions and what the nature of those effects or functions might be. For too many years, the academic left employed a grandiose political vocabulary in what was, in fact, a highly etiolated fashion. There was an embarrassing disparity, as I've pointed out, between the rhetoric of our discourse and its actual effectivity. Typically, the rhetoric had to do with emancipating Fanon's wretched of the earth; the reality had to do with English department meetings.

Back then, it was the conservative backlash to canon reformation that blew hot with the gusty rhetoric of politics. On the right, we heard dire pronouncements about a radical conspiracy to imperil the republic—here, I'd say the *locus classicus* remains George Will's remark that Lynn Cheney's charge, of policing the humanities, was even more imperative to our national security than her husband's charge, as secretary of defense, merely to defend our borders.[5] But there were a thousand variations. In this case, the rhetoric had to do with the end of civilization as we know it, but the reality still had to do with English department meetings.

One of the most agile polemicists of the cultural conservatives, Dinesh D'Souza, urged his fellow conservatives to borrow a leaf from the left and emulate its moral intonations, if not its substance. The rhetoric on the right, he complained, had tended to be the rhetoric of cynicism. The rhetoric on the left, he noted, was the rhetoric of righteous indignation. That tone of righteous indignation, he concluded rather cynically, was precisely what conservatives had to borrow. Having little stomach myself for extended bouts of self-righteousness, I might have been inclined to say, "Take it away; it's all yours." But the fact is, they already had. And if you don't believe me, you missed the GOP convention that year (and in 1996, in 2000, in 2004, and, especially, in Sarah Palin's stunningly powerful revitalization of these old animosities in the Republican National Convention of 2008).

To be sure, the conversion of academic debates into media hype and campaign fodder had, by the summer of 1992, enjoyed more than a running start. When President George H. W. Bush, speaking in 1991 at the University of Michigan, warned against the rampaging threat of "political correctness," he was, it turns out, merely upholding a venerable presidential tradition. As historian Maurice Isserman reminds us, Calvin Coolidge had had much the same thing to say. In the spring of 1921, Vice President Calvin Coolidge warned that radicalism was "infecting women's colleges" "under a cloak of academic freedom." To bolster his thesis, he cited alarming quotes from student newspapers at Smith, Barnard, Bryn Mawr, and elsewhere. The result, Coolidge concluded, was "the ultimate breaking down of the old sturdy virtues of manhood and womanhood, the insidious destruction of character, the weakening of the moral fiber of the individual, the destruction of the foundations of civilization."[6] No doubt much has changed since 1921, and yet those menacing, minor-key organ tones that suffuse Coolidge's prose—the grim forecast of the end of civilization as we know it—remain familiar to the point of banality.

The ironies abound. Freedom of expression, which once had been a reliable issue for the left, became a rallying banner on the right. Whereas once the academic left had stood accused of jockeying for victim status, we found that the right had taken over the vocabulary of victimization and oppression, depicting themselves as lonely martyrs to the jackal hordes of "PC." As a result, the debate frequently degenerated into a sort of playground posturing, more appropriate to *Pee Wee's Playhouse* than the *MacNeil Lehrer News Hour*: "You're hegemonic." "No, *you're* hegemonic." "I know you are, but what am I?" I believe this fairly summarizes several reams of learned prose upon the subject.

The other peculiar feature of the so-called PC debate was that few people on the defense could be described as "pro" political correctness. Conversely, those most actively opposed to political correctness often appeared to be advocates of political correctness in its other ideological flavors. For in another venerable American tradition, ideology is always what the other guy has. Politics is short for the wrong politics. (As the old joke has it, "I have convictions, you have politics, and he has ideology.") Now when William Bennett, as secretary of education, actively campaigned for curricular change, defended such change on political grounds, and enlisted the political capital of the White House to that end, you might be forgiven for thinking that he was, well, politicizing the curriculum. But Bennett would have been quick to set you straight: A politicized curriculum was just what he was opposing. (Do you remember the days of the Vietnam War when we sometimes had to destroy a village in order to save it? I think there's a similar logic at work here.)

At a time when liberalism became the unspeakable "L word," it was bemusing to hear conservatives insist, from well-upholstered positions in the policy

establishment, that PC was enjoying some sort of pernicious ascendancy in the political realm. PC, which
began life as a facetious term of self-parody, became
enlisted in political battles that had very little to do
with what actually happened in the academy. It took
on a life of its own. So that one is tempted to dismiss
the whole thing as a chimera. And of course it wasn't.
The academy does breed orthodoxies, on the left and
the right alike, and it is particularly true that the left
cannot survive without self-criticism. I emphasize
the left only because, having been isolated from actual
power for so long, it has tended to lose touch with
the practicalities of power. After all, in the grand theater of American politics, the "left" is shorthand for
"left out."

The Free Speech Movement: The Sequel

I think it is also true that some figures on the academic/
cultural left too quickly adopted the strategies of
the political right. Here, I'm thinking principally of
the somewhat shopworn debate over "hate speech"
as a variance from protected expression, and it may
be a topic worth reviewing because the question of
free speech has surfaced as the right increasingly em-
ploys blackface caricature in parodies of Barack Obama.

As Michael Kinsley once pointed out, most college statutes restricting freedom of expression were implemented by conservative forces in the early 1970s. Under the banner of "civility," their hope was to control campus radicals who seized on free speech as a shield for their own activities. (Remember the Free Speech movement? Dates you, doesn't it?) Today, ironically, the existence of these same statutes is cited as evidence of a marauding threat from the thought police on the left.

At the very least, I think the convergence of tactics from one era to another ought to give us pause. Another example of such uncomfortable convergences: In drafting legislation to constrain the National Endowment of the Arts, Senator Jesse Helm's office borrowed language from an anti–hate speech statute from (I believe) the University of Wisconsin. If you were wondering why Senator Helms was so intent that the NEA not fund art that could be seen as demeaning to the handicapped, you have your answer. In a similar arena, anti-pornography activists such as Andrea Dworkin and Catherine MacKinnon found themselves working in alliance with conservative municipal groups around the country, and in Canada, at least, the Supreme Court promulgated their sweeping definition of obscenity as the law of the land.

Let me be clear on one point: I am very sensitive to the issues raised in the arguments for hate speech bans. Growing up in a segregated mill town in Appalachia, I sometimes thought there was a sign on my back saying, "Nigger," because that's what some white people seemed to think my name was. So I don't deny that the language of racial prejudice can inflict harm. At the same time—as the Stephen Sondheim song has it—"I'm still here."

The strongest argument for speech bans are, when you examine them more closely, arguments *against* arguments against speech bans. They are often very clever, often persuasive. But what they don't establish is that all things considered, a ban on hate speech is so indispensable, so essential to avoid some present danger, that it justifies handing opponents on the right a gift-wrapped, bow-tied, and beribboned rallying point. In the current environment of symbolic politics, especially with our first African American sleeping in the master bedroom of the White House, the speech ban is a powerful thing: It can turn a garden variety bigot into a First Amendment martyr.

My concern is, first and foremost, a practical one. The problem with speech codes is that they make it impossible to challenge bigotry without it turning into a debate over the right to speak. And that is too great a price to pay. If someone calls me a nigger, I don't want to have to spend the next five hours debating the fine points of John Stuart Mill. Speech codes kill critique. For me, that's what it comes down to.

Given the fact that verbal harassment is already, and uncontroversially, legally proscribed, given the fact, too, that campus speech bans are rarely enforced, the question arises, Do you need them? Their proponents say yes—but they almost always offer *expressive*, rather than *consequentialist*, arguments for them. That is, they do not say, for instance, that the statute will spare vulnerable students some foreseeable amounts of psychic trauma. They say, rather, that by adopting such a statute, the university *expresses* its opposition to hate speech and bigotry. The statute symbolizes our commitment to tolerance, to the creation of an educational environment where mutual colloquy and comity are preserved.

Well, yes, this sounds like a nice thing to symbolize. What we forget is that once we have retreated to the level of symbolic, gestural politics, we have to take into account all the other symbolic considerations. So even if you think that the free speech position contains logical holes and inconsistency, you need to register *its* symbolic force. And it is this level of scrutiny that tips the balance in the other direction.

Now, I remember thinking at the time that the PC debate was beginning to wear thin; that the apocalyptic, Wagnerian rhetoric was beginning to sound a little over-rehearsed; that those ominous minor-key organ tones were beginning to lose their ability to send chills down our spine. And I, for one, was not sorry in the least, partly because I regarded the PC hysteria as a form of the politics of distraction. Literary scholar John Guillory wryly remarked at the time: "If liberal pluralism has discovered that the cultural is always also the political (which it is), it has seldom escaped the trap of reducing the political to the cultural."[7]

Unfortunately, the tendency is scarcely confined to liberal pluralists. It is now, almost twenty years after Buchanan's curiously seminal speech, common property across the political spectrum. Worrying about the political tendencies of the New Historicism, for example, makes it easier to lose sight of what is happening on the streets outside—where more than a third of all black children still live below the poverty line and a black male in his twenties is still more likely to end up in jail, in prison, or on parole than in college, just as was true in 1992. As a black scholar, I cannot forget that for the astonishing percentage of African Americans who were functionally illiterate then—

who remain functionally illiterate now—the debate over the canon had, and continues to have, all the relevance that an argument over interior decoration has for a homeless person.

Cultural Literacy: The Sequel

But if the PC debate turned out to be about less than met the eye, and if presidential and vice-presidential scare-mongering over cultural elites and academic radicals was of uncertain consequence as the 1990s progressed, how are we to gauge the political stakes of the culture wars?

Closest to hand, on this score, are the arguments put forward by E. D. Hirsch in connection to his "cultural literacy" project. Essentially, Hirsch suggested that by establishing a base of common knowledge, our schools could better produce citizens able to participate on an equal footing in the common polity. His may be our generation's most Emersonian vision of civic society, in which some minimum core of shared knowledge is important for political empowerment. So what we have here is an anti-elitist, democratizing impulse. The primary beneficiaries Hirsch said he had in mind were the so-called underprivileged, those relatively marginalized from the exercise of power, those for whom the school environment was the main site of transmission of "cultural literacy," which is, by stipulation, also political literacy.

What political advantages are conferred by cultural literacy—a knowledge of the common core? There are more and less elaborate explanations, but the short answer is that it's a matter of "catching the references." As anyone who learns another language is repeatedly reminded, a crude word knowledge isn't sufficient properly to understand a text; you need to know something of the rich texture of conventional allusions—"to be or not to be," that sort of thing. And so it is with discourse from our political leaders, which an informed citizenry must assess.

For better or worse, however, the patterns of references have changed significantly from Abraham Lincoln's day, and Hirsch's vision of the texture of political discourse was embarrassingly generous, as if his model of a modern political figure were confined to Daniel Patrick Moynihan. Similarly, Vice President Quayle, scourge of the cultural elite, announced in 1992 that the presidential campaign would really be about *character*. It quickly emerged that what he meant was *characters*—the Waltons, Bart Simpson, Murphy Brown. There's nothing very new here. About all I can remember of the 1988 presidential campaign were George Bush's reference to *Jake and the Fat Man* and Michael Dukakis's to Joe Isuzu. (Hirsch was widely condemned when he explained that to attain cultural literacy, you didn't actually have to read any of William Shakespeare's plays, just recognize the allusions to them. Strangely, no one seemed too alarmed when Bush conceded he'd never seen *Jake and the Fat Man* and Dan Quayle admitted that he'd never watched an episode of *Murphy Brown*, thus taking the Hirschian principle to a self-denying extreme.)

In the public discourse of national politics, then, we waited in vain for the allusion to Shakespeare or any of his characters. Somehow we managed to discuss the vacillating Ross Perot with nary a mention of Hamlet, candidate Bill Clinton with no side glance at Romeo, and the first President Bush with scarcely a thought of King Lear. (Granted, the Clarence Thomas–Anita Hill hearings were an exception to this pattern, being a veritable orgy of Shakespeareana; I can't explain why, but for more than a few senators, Othello loomed dark and inescapable in their minds. But this I take to be the exception that proves the rule.)

By contrast, Quayle weighed in on Tupac Shakur, then the lead rapper of the group Digital Underground, and I fully expected George H. W. Bush to pronounce on Madonna's latest shrink-wrapped endeavor at any time. (Otherwise, high art surfaced into public consciousness only if it had been denied a grant from the NEA.) In short, Hirsch's *Cultural Literacy* projected a rather fetchingly idealized image of political colloquy, one quaintly removed from the all-pervasive flux of mass culture. The truth is, we do not require a book on cultural literacy to inform us about the *actual* referents of political discourse today; a subscription to *Vanity Fair* or *Entertainment Weekly* will do quite nicely.

So it turns out that the democratizing aspect of mass culture—also known as "market penetration"—may have supplanted, to some degree, the role played by the school and by school culture in the dissemination of what we could call "political literacy." If we want to assess the political stakes of the culture wars, in Pat Buchanan's day and in ours, we may have to look elsewhere.

Multiculturalism: The Sequel

At this point, it may help to focus on one especially populous arena of the cultural wars, that associated with the rubric of "multiculturalism." What happens when the Vandals and Visigoths—as Buchanan put it—start asking for equal time? What happens when the barbarians within seek full participation in the cultural as well as the civic domain of the nation? Of course, we would do ourselves a disservice to allow a Buchanan to set the terms of argument, and I shall not.

In what follows, I want to pursue the paradoxes of pluralism, and because the grounds will soon grow muddier, let me set out a blueprint of the critical overview that's to come. In an unpardonably abbreviated fashion, I want to elicit some of the tensions that were internal to—not all, but some—versions of multiculturalism concerning identity and liberation and concerning multiculturalism's so-called relativism (something that, I argue, any cogent multiculturalism must repudiate). I want to probe some of the limitations of multiculturalism, which is to say multi*culturalism* as a *model* for the range of phenomena it has often been required to subsume, and I want to raise questions about the triumph, the historically recent triumph, of ethnicity (so called) as a paradigm or master code for human difference. In other words, I want to take seriously multiculturalism's critics on the left as well as the right. And then I want to search for something multiculturalism has sometimes been supposed to lack, namely, and perhaps ironically, a coherent political vision. Leapfrogging, improbably enough, from Frantz Fanon to Isaiah Berlin, I conclude with an appeal for pluralism, but a pluralism, let me serve fair notice, of a singularly banal and uninspiring variety, conducing to a vision of society, and of the university, as a place of what one philosopher calls "constrained disagreement." To coin a phrase, then, this will be two cheers for multiculturalism. Sorry, now that I've told you how this ends, I guess I've ruined the suspense. On the other hand, forewarned *is* forearmed.

The Limits of Culturalism

The first thing we usually do when we set out to discuss an issue seriously is to narrow the subject in some useful way, to say that this is, and that is not, what we're talking about. One difficulty raised by the variety of uses to which this thing called multiculturalism has been put is that multiculturalism itself has certain imperial tendencies. We know it is concerned with the representation of difference. The question naturally arises, Whose differences and which differences? Almost all differences in which we take an interest express themselves in cultural ways; many, perhaps most, are indeed exhausted by their cultural manifestations. To assert this is, in most cases, to assert a tautology. At this point, we might move in a little further and say that multiculturalism is concerned with the representation, not of difference as such, but of cultural identities. We might ask, then, What *sorts* of identities are helpfully modeled by multiculturalism? The answer is less than obvious. Gender identity, sexual identity, racial identity: if all these things are socially inflected and produced, rather than unmediatedly natural, why won't they fit into the culturalist model? Or will they?

We can probably agree, for example, that gender identity and sexual identity are hard to reduce to the model of cultural difference, even though the meanings of these categories are culturally specific. First, these are categories we can discuss in a trans-cultural, trans-historical manner if only to elaborate on their trans-cultural and trans-historical disparities. (Try that with "Basque" or "Catalan." The very idea, needless to say, is unintelligible.) Second, though, the culturalist model (and I'm using culturalism in a context-specific and anomalous way, as a back formation from multiculturalism) normally thinks in terms of cultural bubbles that may collide but usually could, in principle, exist in splendid isolation from one another (I touch on reasons for this later). Hence the rubric of

"cultural diversity." This sort of cultural externalism—
required by a model of cultural distance or disparity—
does not work so well in the case of gender identity
or sexual identity. Difference, yes, but a difference
within, something, as it were, culturally intrinsic. Why
won't the culturalist reduction work? As Jonathan
Dollimore once pointed out in the case of sexual difference, homophobia in our culture is part of the
structure of sexuality itself. So it's not, as it were, out
there; it's in here. Othering, as I've said elsewhere, starts
in the home. So, too, sexism, perhaps even more obviously, is part of our conventional gender identities.

Which isn't to deny the existence of subcultural
differentia in particular social contexts, wherein sexual
difference seems to become, as it were, "ethnicized"
and a sexual ethnicity is forged. At the same time, the
relation between the sexual and the cultural is necessarily contingent. Obviously, we can't assume that
Ronald Firbank and Sophocles or, for that matter,
Marcel Proust and Michelangelo would recognize
their putative fraternity.

And yet it has sometimes seemed to me that what
really explained the fervor of some of the Afrocentrist
preoccupation with Egypt was an unexpressed belief
that very deep continuities supervene upon skin color.
So beyond the heartfelt claim that Cleopatra was

"black" was the lurking conviction that if you traveled back in time and dropped the needle on a James Brown album, Cleo would instantly break out into the Camel Walk. The hope and belief that we cherish is not so much a proposition about melanin and physiognomy; it's the proposition that beneath the scales of time and through the mists of history Cleopatra was a *sister*.

For obvious reasons, sexual dimorphism is a quite basic aspect of human experience; racial difference is certainly less so. Understanding its significance always requires a particular engagement with a specific historical trajectory. There is no master key. But what emerges, again, is that, despite the very complex interrelations between race and culture—a matter that takes a sinister turn in the racialization of culture in the nineteenth century—no ready conversion factor connects the two, only the vagaries of history.

As critic John Brenkman notes, in an important essay to which I return, African Americans have been inscribed in the American matrix in a particular way. It's not merely that they are missing or absent or elsewhere: "Blacks were historically not merely excluded from the American polity; they were inscribed within it as nonparticipants." He continues: "The forms of that negating inscription have varied through a complex history of legal and political designations. These set the conditions of the African-American discourse on identity and citizenship, and the meaning of that discourse would in turn have to be interpreted in light of those conditions and of the strategies embedded in its response to them."[8] (Later on, we see how race complicates even Brenkman's own sketch of a multicultural polity.)

What good are roots, Gertrude Stein once remarked, if you can't take them with you? But a number of critics now suggest that the contemporary model of ethnicity sometimes fails us by its historically foreshortened perspective, its inability to grasp the roots as well as the branches of cultural identity. As early as 1992, theorist E. San Juan harshly decried what he called the "cult of ethnicity and the fetish of pluralism" and launched probably the most thoroughgoing critique of multiculturalism from a radical perspective we had before Bill Clinton became president. "With the gradual institutionalization/academicization of Ethnic Studies," San Juan wrote, "'the cult of ethnicity' based on the paradigm of European immigrant success became the orthodox doctrine. The theoretical aggrandizement of ethnicity systematically erased from the historical frame of reference any perception of race and racism as causal factors in the making of the political and economic structure of the United States."[9] In a similar vein, Hazel Carby proposed that "insisting that 'culture' denotes antagonistic relations of domination and subordination . . . undermines the pluralistic notion of compatibility inherent in *multi*culturalism." She continued: "The paradigm of multiculturalism actually excludes the concept of dominant and subordinate cultures—either indigenous or migrant—and fails to recognize that the existence of racism relates to the possession and exercise of politico-economic control and authority and also to forms of resistance to the power of dominant social groups."[10] (Later on, we see how some versions of emancipation are in conflict with some versions of identity politics.)

I want to take up some of the issues raised here, but I want to make an aside as well because it strikes me that a failure to engage with radical critiques of this sort has been a characteristic of liberal multiculturalism and an impoverishing one. Those familiar with multiculturalism only through its right-wing opponents are sometimes surprised to discover that these broadly gauged radical critiques even existed. And as I've remarked elsewhere, I think the extended face-off with conservatism has had its deforming effects; what you can sometimes end up with is a multiculturalism that knows what it's against but not what it's *for*. So even if we finally demur from aspects of the radical critique, we will be better off for having sorted through these arguments. Spoken—I can hear the put-down already—like a true liberal. End of aside.

In any event, as a rather mundane demonstration of the way in which the multiculturalistic paradigm tends even today to occlude race, I suggest that each of you perform the following little test. When you read the newspaper, take careful note of the way the word "multicultural" is used. In a column on advertising, a Benetton's ad with black and white and Asian children together will be described as "multicultural." But do these children—presumably supplied by the Ford Modeling Agency and in all likelihood hailing from exotic Westchester County—in fact represent different cultures? That, of course, is the one thing you cannot tell from a photograph of this sort. But I think you will find that in every instance where the older form "multiracial" would have been used, the newer lexeme "multicultural" is employed instead, even where cultural traits, as opposed to physiognomic traits, are obviously undiscoverable or irrelevant.

Now, I want to be clear. In many, many cases, the shift from race to ethnicity was a salutary one, a necessary move away from the essentialist biologizing of a previous era. The emphasis on the social construction of race may be a familiar one, but it remains an imperative one for all that. And yet we ought to consider the correlative danger of essentializing culture when we blithely allow culture to substitute for race without affecting the basic circulation of the term. In a conventional multicultural vision, for every insult there is a culture: that is, if I can be denigrated as an X, I can be affirmed as an X. Perhaps not the most sophisticated mechanism of remediation, but the intentions are good.

So far, we've seen the ethnicity paradigm faulted for a tendency to leave out history, power relations, and, of course, the history of power relations. But its perplexities do not end here. We might bear in mind that the ascent of the vocabulary of ethnicity is, as Werner Sollors has emphasized, largely a post-war phenomenon, the very term having been coined by W. Lloyd Warner in 1941. It may be that what's most conservative about some populist versions of multiculturalism is an understanding of group identity and groups rights that borrows whole hog a reified conception of cultural membership borrowed from the social sciences of midcentury. What's new is that cultural survival—the preservation of cultural differentia—is assigned an almost medical sense of urgency. And if the delimitation of cultural identity borrows from the social sciences, the interpretation of its products sometimes seems to court the gaze of anthropology; in place of hermeneutics, it would seem, some might prefer ethnography.

Then there's another paradox. In a critique of liberal individualism, we decry the instability of the individual as a category, and yet we sometimes reconstitute and recuperate the same essential stability in the form of a "group" that allegedly exhibits the same regularities and uniformities we could not locate in the individual subject. Conversely, as John Guillory writes, "the critique of the canon responds to the disunity of the culture as a whole, as a fragmented whole, by constituting new cultural unities at the level of gender, race, or more recently, ethnic subcultures, or gay or lesbian subcultures."[11] Perhaps in this vein, John Brenkman ventures that "the neoconservative and neoliberal mania for insisting that all questions regarding citizenship merely concern individuals as individuals, not as members of social groups, is a bid to forestall struggles over these social requirements of citizenship."[12] Skepticism about the status of the individual is surely chastening, but there may be a danger in a too easy invocation of the correlative group, the status of which may be problematic in another way.

Finally, to complete our overview of the limits of culturalism, we should take account of the critique of multiculturalism put forward by influential French anthropologist Jean-Loup Amselle, who contends that the very notion of discrete ethnicities is an artifact of his discipline. Warning against what he dubs ethnic or cultural fundamentalism, Amselle maintains that the notion of a multicultural society, "far from being an instrument of tolerance and of liberation of minorities, as its partisans affirm, manifests, to the contrary, all the hallmarks of ethnological reason, and that is why it has been taken up in France by the New Right." But Amselle's concerns are not merely political; they are ontological as well. "Cultures aren't situated one by the other like Leibniz's windowless monads," he argues. Rather, "the very definition of a given culture is in fact the result of intercultural relations of forces."[13] On the face of it, Amselle's considerations are yet another blow against what I've referred to as the bubble model of cultures. Insofar as this was a necessary feature of the culturalism promoted by multiculturalism, it might have to be discarded. I return to this challenge a little later.

Identity Versus Politics

Even though the discourse of identity politics and that of liberation are often conflated, on a more fundamental level they may be in a mortal combat. Identity politics in its purest form must be concerned with the survival of an *identity*. By contrast, the utopian agenda of liberation pursues what it takes to be the objective interests of its subjects, but may be little concerned with cultural continuity or integrity. More than that, the discourse of liberation often hinges on the birth of a transformed subject, the creation of a new identity, which is, by definition, the surcease of the old. And that, at least in theory, is the rub.

To take an example I touched on in Chapter 3, if colonialism, let us say, inscribes itself upon the psyche of the colonized, if it is part of the process of colonial subject formation, then doesn't this establish limits to the very intelligibility of liberation? That, more or less, was the critique that, as we have seen, Tunisian philosopher Albert Memmi made about the would-be Algerian Fanon's anti-colonial rhetoric. After all, how are we to prize apart the discourse of the colonized from the discourse of the colonizer? Recall that Memmi suggested that Fanon—for all his own ambivalences—somehow believed that "the day oppression ceases, the new man is supposed to appear before our eyes immediately." But, Memmi reminded us, "this is not the way it happens." The utopian moment that Memmi decries in Fanon is in his depiction of decolonization as engendering "a kind of tabula rasa," as "quite simply the replacing of a certain 'species' of men by another 'species' of men," so that the fear that we will continue to be (as he puts it) "overdetermined from without" was never reconciled with his political vision of emancipation. Certainly, it would be hard to reconcile with any recognizable version of identitarian politics.

And it's a lesson we can easily retrieve from the hot sands of Algeria. Any discourse of emancipation, insofar as it retains a specifically cultural cast, must contend with similar issues. That's the paradox entailed by a politics conducted on behalf of cultural identities when those identities are in part defined by the structural or positional features that the politics aims to dismantle.

Return, for a moment, to Carby's insistence that the "paradigm of multiculturalism actually excludes the concept of dominant and subordinate cultures." Is this so? Or, rather, in what sense is this so? I think Guillory, whose work on the canon debate was plainly the best of its kind, provides the gloss when he writes that "a culturalist politics, though it glances worriedly at the phenomenon of class, has in practice never devised a politics that would specifically address class 'identity.' For a while it is easy enough to conceive of a self-affirmative racial or sexual identity, it makes very little sense to posit an affirmative lower-class identity, as such an identity would have to be grounded in the experience of deprivation per se," the affirmation of which is "hardly incompatible with a program for the abolition of want."[14] And yet class may provide just a particularly stark instance of a more general limitation. Obviously, if being subordinate were a constitutive aspect of an identity, then a liberation politics would foreclose identity politics, and vice versa. Such is stipulatively the case for Guillory's example of a "lower-class identity." But might it not, at least contingently, prove the case for a host of other putatively "cultural" identities as well?

The point I want to return to is that identity politics cannot be understood as a politics in the harness of a pre-given identity. The "identity" half of the catchall phrase "identity politics" must be conceived as equally labile and dynamic as the "politics" half. The two terms must be in dialogue, as it were. Otherwise, we should be prepared for the phrase to be revealed to be an oxymoron.

Multiculturalism and Democracy

Having taken note of the ways in which identity and politics may actually be in battle with each other, we might now ask how the two are best reconciled. Can multiculturalism—often depicted as a slippery slope to anarchy and tribal war—actually support the sort of civil society we might want? Given my skeptical account of the temptations of political posturing, I think I had better proceed modestly here, reining in the rhetoric as best I can.

Distinguished historian John Higham once complained that "multiculturalism has remained for two decades a stubbornly practical enterprise, a movement within an overall theory, justified by urgent group needs rather than long range goals. . . . Still, it is troubling that twenty years after those convulsive beginnings, multiculturalism has suddenly become [in the early 1990s] a policy issue in America's colleges, universities, and secondary schools without yet proposing a vision of the kind of society it wants."[15] Multiculturalism may or may not have political consequences, in Higham's rather persuasive diagnosis, but it did not have a political vision.

What makes John Brenkman's essay on the subject among the most intriguing I've read is that it took up Higham's challenge, explicitly addressing what we might, to coin a phrase, call the "vision thing." For this reason, I think it repays a certain amount of attention.

In a provocative and unusual attempt to connect the multicultural agenda to the program of democracy, Brenkman argues that

> citizens can freely enter the field of political persuasion and decision only insofar as they draw on the contingent vocabularies of their own identities. Democracy needs participants who are conversant with the images, symbols, stories and vocabularies that have evolved across the whole of the history. . . . By the same token, democracy also requires citizens who are fluent enough in one another's vocabularies and histories to share the forums of political deliberation and decision on an equal footing.[16]

I find this an attractive and heartening formulation, even if, in its instrumental conception of cultural knowledge, it may have unsuspected affinities with E. D. Hirsch. But there are two other points I want to draw out here. First, a caveat: To say that citizens can "freely enter the field of political persuasion and decision"—which is to say, the field of politics, *tout court*—"only insofar as they draw on the contingent vocabularies of their own identities" is to suppose that one exists, in some sense, as a cultural atom, that one's identity exists anterior to one's engagement in the field of the political. It is to suppose that one arrives to this field already constituted, already culturally whole, rather than acknowledging (as I think Brenkman does move toward later on) that the political might itself create or contour one's cultural or ethnic identity. Second, though, notice that this formulation does not itself entail what we might call "group" multiculturalism, which is devoted to the empowerment of crisply delimited cultural units, and which conceives society as a sort of federation of officially recognized cultural sovereignties. We've already registered the sorts of criticisms that have been raised against the model, but they needn't arise just yet.

Brenkman is no Pangloss. He remarks a tension between multiculturalism and democracy, but he proposes a tradition of civic republicanism or civic humanism by which the tension might be resolved. The emphasis of this tradition, which was a particular influence in the early history of this republic, is on civic participation over liberalism's privatism; individual development (here he cites British historian J. G. A. Pocock) is seen as intrinsically linked to a person's participation as a citizen of an "autonomous decision-making community, a polis or republic."[17] Even so, Brenkham concedes, civic humanism also always assumed the homogeneity of those who enjoyed citizenship. As Michael Warner has shown, for example, the republican representation of citizenship in revolutionary America tacitly depended upon the exclusion of women, African slaves, and Native Americans from the forms of literacy that were the emblem and the means of the patriots' equality. To evoke the republican tradition in the context of multicultural societies quickly exposes those elements of civic humanism that run directly counter to diversity and plurality.[18]

The charge that this civic humanism depended on the homogeneity of its citizenry is easily supported, but is *cultural* homogeneity precisely the issue? As I noted before, the exclusion of women is not, at least customarily, depicted as a matter of cultural distance. And although both Native Americans and African slaves *would* doubtless be marked by cultural differentia, what was criticized here, recall, was the perpetuation of such difference by the withholding of the tools of assimilation, namely, English literacy.

What is at stake is *not* the eradication of difference—by, for example, the unwanted *imposition* of English literacy, which is a grievance that has arisen in some non-Western settings. We cannot, then, conclude that *cultural* distance motivated the exclusion of African slaves and Native Americans; on the contrary, their exclusion was achieved by enforcing their cultural distance. And so what we come up against, once again, are the limits of the culturalist model, its tendency to occlude the categories of race.

However symptomatic these slippages—and I cite them as cautionary—I believe Brenkman's elaborated vision of the "modern polity [as] a dynamic space in which citizenship is always being contested rather than the fixed space of the pre-modern ideal of a republic" was a signal contribution to the debate surrounding multiculturalism.[19]

Multiculturalism Versus Relativism

One last obstacle remains to the articulation of a multicultural polity, and that is the specter of relativism, which continues to haunt many of multiculturalism's friends and outrages its enemies. For the cultural conservatives, from William Kristol and Roger Kimball to Rush Limbaugh and Sarah Palin, it has totemic significance, a one-word encapsulation of all that is wrong with their progressive counterparts. If all difference deserves respect, how can morality survive and governance be maintained? Progressives find the doctrine equally unsettling: The righting of wrongs, after all, demands a recognition of them *as* wrongs. And the classic 1965 handbook by Herbert Marcuse, Barrington Moore, and Robert Paul Wolff, *A Critique of Pure Tolerance*, should remind us that critiques from the left are far from exceptional. Indeed, it seems scarcely plausible that relativism has anything like the currency that some critics have imputed to it. "'Relativism,'" Richard Rorty has stated, "is the view that every belief on a certain topic, or perhaps about *any* topic is as good as every other. No one holds this view," he says flatly, except, he allows, "the occasional cooperative freshman."[20] In truth, as we see, this is an overstatement, though in the present climate, probably a salutary one.

To be sure, relativism comes in many different flavors—moral and aesthetic as well as epistemological—and what actually *follows* from relativism of any particular variety is seldom very clear. But there is one kind of relativism—of the epistemological or cognitive variety (I revisit value relativism later on)—that has achieved a certain limited currency among some anthropologists, whose business is, as it were, culture, and that might be supposed to make an occasional appearance in the multicultural context.

The Wittgensteinian Peter Winch, for example, in his classic book *The Idea of a Social Science and Its Relation to Philosophy*, has argued that "our idea of what belongs to the realm of reality is given to us in the language that we use."[21] John Beattie has decried a similar cognitive relativism in, for example, the writings of F. Allan Hanson (*Meaning in Culture*) and Roy Wagner (*The Invention of Culture*).[22] For Winch, there is no reality independent of our conceptual schemes, which may differ in incommensurable ways.

This is a curious view, one that has been rebutted most vigorously by intellectuals from just those non-Western cultures that relativism would consign to hermetic isolation. As distinguished Ghanaian philosopher Kwasi Wiredu writes: "Relativism . . . falsely denied the existence of interpersonal criteria of rationality. That is what the denial of objectivity amounts to. Unless at least the basic canons of rational thinking were common to men, they could not even communicate among themselves. Thus, in seeking to foreclose rational discussion, the relativist view is in effect seeking to undermine the foundations of human community."[23]

The general problem of relativism of this sort is that it makes the project of cross-cultural understanding unintelligible. (As Martin Hollis observes, "Without assumptions about reality and rationality we cannot translate anything, and no translation could show the assumptions to be wrong.")[24] So let me put the argument at its strongest: If relativism is right, then multiculturalism is impossible. Relativism, far from conducing to multiculturalism, would withdraw its very conditions of possibility.

Pluralism: The Sequel

By way of a return to politics, and a rounding out of my critical overview, I want to enlist Isaiah Berlin, whom we might describe as the paterfamilias of liberal pluralism, and whose utter and complete banishment from the debate was a matter of puzzlement, unless the fear was that adducing Berlin's lifelong argument would compromise our claims to novelty. For Berlin stresses—and, as I say, his is an argument that was largely overlooked in the debate over multiculturalism—that "relativism is not the only alternative to what Lovejoy called uniformitarianism."[25] In what Berlin describes as pluralism, "we are free to criticize the values of other cultures, to condemn them, but we cannot pretend not to understand them at all, or to regard them simply as subjective, the product of creatures in different circumstances with different tastes from our own, which do not speak to us at all."[26] He writes, and because this is one of my favorite passages of his, I'd like to quote him at length:

> What is clear is that values can clash—that is why civilizations are incompatible. They can be incompatible between cultures, or groups in the same culture, or between you and me. . . . Values may easily clash within the breast of a single individual; and it does not follow that, if they do some must be true or others false. [Indeed,] these collisions of values are of the essence of what they are and what we are. If we are told that these contradictions will be solved in some perfect world in which all good things can be harmonized in principle, then we must answer, to those who say this, that the meanings they attach to the names which for us denote the conflicting values are not ours. We must say that the world in which what we see as incompatible values are not in conflict is a world altogether beyond our ken; that principles which are harmonized in this other world are not the principles with which, in our daily lives, we are acquainted; if they are transformed, it is into conceptions not known to us on earth. But it is on

earth that we live, and it is here that we must believe and act.

The notion of the perfect whole, the ultimate solution, in which all good things coexist, seems to me to be not merely unattainable—that is a truism—but conceptually incoherent; I do not know what is meant by a harmony of this kind. Some among the Great Goods cannot live together. That is a conceptual truth. We are doomed to choose, and every choice may entail an irreparable loss.[27]

To be sure, Berlin's pluralism is radically anti-utopian. Perhaps it is not the sort of thing likely to inspire one to risk one's life or the lives of others. But I don't think it is a flaccid or undemanding faith for all that. And in the essay from which I've quoted, entitled "The Pursuit of the Ideal," he anticipates the complaint:

Of course social or political collisions will take place; the mere conflict of positive values alone makes this unavoidable. Yet they can, I believe, be minimized by promoting and preserving an uneasy equilibrium, which is constantly threatened and in need of repair—that alone, I repeat, is the precondition for decent societies and morally acceptable behavior, otherwise we are bound to lose our way. A little dull as a solution, you will say? Not the stuff of which calls to heroic action by inspired leaders are made? Yet if there is some truth in this view, perhaps that is sufficient.[28]

The vision here, if it is a vision, is one of the central themes of Berlin's corpus, but we can find it promulgated elsewhere and with a range of inflections. It warns us off final solutions of all sorts, admonishes us that the search for purity—whether we speak of "ethnic cleansing," of "cantonization," or of "cultural authenticity"—poses a greater threat to civil order, and human decency, than the messy affair of cultural variegation. It lets us remember that identities are always in dialogue, exist (as Amselle expatiates) only in relation to each other, and are, like everything else, sites of contest and negotiation, self-fashioning and refashioning. (As John Higham observes, "An adequate theory of American culture will have to address the reality of assimilation as well as the persistence of differences.")[29] And it suggests, finally, that a multiculturalism that can accept all that—and I see no inherent barriers to it—might be one worth working for.

The not-so-very utopian vision here may correspond to what Alasdair MacIntyre has called for in the present-day university, as a place of "constrained disagreement."[30] Constrained disagreement: It doesn't seem such a daunting ideal, and perhaps not only the university but also the society that supports it should expect to survive by conducting itself in this way. But let me anticipate some concerns.

Have I permitted a benignly folkloristic notion of multiculturalism to preempt a potently oppositional one, "red in tooth and claw"? Here, I'd recommend that these critics on the left remind themselves of the vehement opposition of those on the right to even such concessive pluralism; surely anything that makes Buchanan foam at the mouth can't be all bad. Beyond that, however, I believe we should concede that the radical critics are correct in suspecting multiculturalism as an agency for radical transformation. If you want radical transformation (as opposed, say, to dramatic reform), identity politics probably isn't the place to start and multiculturalism is a veritable quagmire.

Conversely, though, others may wonder, Haven't I discounted too quickly the perils of cultural diversity? On the diversity issue, I meekly suggest that its conservative critics listen to its radical critics: If the issue is half as inert as they say, surely civilization as we know it is all too likely to continue.

The truth is, though, I'm wary of overly schematic responses to these issues. The culture wars have presented us with a surfeit of either/ors. Tradition versus modernity. Separatism versus assimilationism. Monoculturalism versus multiculturalism. Eurocentrism versus Afrocentrism. Communitarianism versus individualism. Rights versus responsibilities. My culture versus your culture.

It seems to me that if the discourse of multiculturalism can yield a lasting benefit, it would be to steer us away from these mindless dichotomies. For we've become demoralized by the crude reductive side-taking on the debate. It's gotten so I can't find anyone not already *in* the debate who wants to identify with either side! Down with either/or. Up with both/and. Both rights and responsibilities. Both tradition and modernity. Both your culture and mine. And they will conflict, these things we cherish; they will jostle and collide against one another, and these clashes will determine and define who we are.

There is a war going on, Pat Buchanan told us, incredibly, almost twenty years ago, in the words with which I began this chapter, a war "for the soul of America." I think there's a sense in which Buchanan was right. There was, and continues to be, such a cultural war going on, and, indeed, there always has been. (In words uncannily similar, the liberal Charles M. Blow has argued that the cultural right's rage at Obama is just one face of "the current fight for the soul of this country. It's not just a tug of war between the mind and the heart, between evidence and emotions, between reason and anger, between what we know and believe."[31] But when Buchanan said that the war was for the soul of America, he misspoke. This war, as it continues even at a length and in forms that we could not possibly have imagined in the early 1990s, is not for the soul of America. This war *is* the soul of America.

Acknowledgments

I would like to thank Kwame Anthony Appiah, Bennett Ashley, Houston and Charlotte Baker, Homi K. Bhabha, Tina Brown, Ross Curley, Angela De Leon, Henry Finder, Philip Fisher, Candace Heineman, Barbara Johnson, Isaac Julien, Joanne Kendall, Sieglinde Lemke, Kobena Mercer, W. J. T. Mitchell, Renee Mussai, Julian Pavia, Frank H. Pearl, Brandon Proia, Hollis Robbins, Elaine Scarry, Mark Sealy, Meredith Smith, Jennifer Snodgrass, Shirley Sun, Abby Wolf, Donald Yacovone, and the Faculty of English at the University of Oxford.

Notes

Preface

1. Charles M. Blow, "An Article of Faith," *New York Times*, April 3, 2010, p. A17.

Chapter One: Enlightenment's Esau

1. Quoted in James Baldwin, "Princes and Powers," in *The Price of the Ticket: Collected Nonfiction, 1948–1985* (New York: St. Martin's Press, 1985), 44.

2. Richard Wright, "Tradition and Industrialization: The Plight of the Tragic Elite in Africa," *Présence Africaine*, nos. 8–10 (June–November 1956): 348.

3. Ibid., 355.

4. Ibid., 356.

5. Ibid., 357.

6. Ibid., 356, 358.

7. Ibid., 358, 359, 360.

8. Baldwin, "Princes and Powers," 59.

9. See Addison Gayle, ed., *The Black Aesthetic* (Garden City, NY: Doubleday, 1971).

10. Wright, "Tradition and Industrialization," 356.

11. "Débats—20 Septembre, á 21 h.," *Présence Africaine*, nos. 8–10 (June–November 1956): 217.

12. Wright provided his own prehistory for the "mood of objectivity," although this bit does not appear in the *White Man, Listen* version: "Some few thousand years ago somewhere in the mountains of Greece, a mood overcame some poor Greek hunter or farmer. Instead of the world that he saw being full of life born of his own psychological projections, it suddenly happened that he saw it bleakly and bluntly for what it was. The mood of objectivity was born and we do not know on what date. But we find its reality in Greek life and in Greek art" ("Tradition and Industrialization," 353). Presumably this vision of the disenchantment of the world is to be counterposed to the mystified universe of the non-Westernized African. In an apparent concession, he wrote: "The most rigorously determined attitude of objectivity is, at best, relative. We are human; we are slaves of time and circumstance; we are the victims of our passions and illusions" (349). But to say that we are victims of our passions and illusions and history is not the same as to say that these things constitute who we are. To say we are victims of them is surely to posit that anterior ahistorical subject to which distorting circumstances are likely to affect, but for which we can try to compensate.

13. "Débats," 217.

14. Baldwin, *The Price of the Ticket*, 51.

15. Paul Gilroy, "Cruciality and the Frog's Perspective," in *Small Acts: Thoughts on the Politics of Black Cultures* (London: Serpent's Tail, 1993), 109.

16. Edmund Burke, letter to French Laurence, 28 July 1796, in *The Correspondence of Edmund Burke*, ed. H. Furber et al., 10 vols. (Cambridge: Cambridge University Press, 1958–1965), 9:62.

17. Burke, "Speech on Mr. Fox's East-India Bill," in *The Works of the Right Honourable Edmund Burke,* by Edmund Burke, 12 vols. (Boston, 1889; hereafter referred to as *Works*), 2:434.

18. Burke, *Works,* 11:158.

19. Ibid., 10:85, 9:458.

20. Burke, letter to Philip Francis, February 23, 1785, in *The Correspondence,* 5:245.

21. See the discussion of Burke's misappropriations in Isaac Kramnick, *The Rage of Burke: Portrait of an Ambivalent Conservative* (New York: Basic Books, 1977), which advances a conception of Burke as an "ambivalent radical."

22. Quoted in Sunil Kumar Sen, "Introduction," to *Edmund Burke on Indian Economy,* ed. Sunil Kumar Sen (Calcutta: Calcutta Progressive Publishers, 1969), i–xvii.

23. Karl Marx, *Capital: A Critique of Political Economy,* trans. Ben Fowkes, 3 vols. (Harmondsworth, UK: Penguin, 1976), 1:926n13, 440.

24. Karl Marx, "The British Rule in India," in *Basic Writings on Politics and Philosophy,* by Karl Marx and Friedrich Engels, ed. Lewis Feuer (Garden City, NY: Doubleday, 1959), 480.

25. Ibid., 480, 481.

26. *The History of the Trial of Warren Hastings, Esq., Late Governor-General of Bengal* (London: Debrett, 1796), 8.

27. Stuart Hall, "Race and Moral Panics in Post-war Britain," in *Five Views of Multi-racial Britain: Talks on Race Relations Broadcast by BBC TV* (London: Commission for Racial Equality, 1987); cited in Paul Gilroy, "Stepping Out of Babylon—Race, Class, and Autonomy," in *The Empire Strikes Back: Race and Racism in 70s Britain,* by Paul Gilroy et al. (London: CCCS/Hutchinson, 1982), 284.

28. James Mill, *The History of British India*, 6 vols. (London, 1820), 5:232.

29. Thomas Babington Macaulay, *Speeches by Lord Macaulay, with His "Minute on Indian Education,"* ed. G. M. Young (London: Oxford University Press, 1935), 349.

30. Baldwin, "Princes and Powers," 51.

31. Burke, *Works*, 1:192.

32. Kramnick, *The Rage of Edmund Burke*, 8.

33. Burke, letter to Richard Shackleton, 25 May 1779, in *The Correspondence*, 4:80.

34. Kramnick, *The Rage of Edmund Burke*, 84.

35. Burke, *Works*, 12:31.

36. Edmund Burke, *A Note-Book of Edmund Burke*, ed. H. V. F. Somerset (Cambridge: Cambridge University Press, 1957), 71.

37. You might think this would be a point of affinity with Wright's "scientific" outlook, but in fact the lexeme "nature" plays a multivalent role in Wright's address. "Being a Negro living in a white Western Christian society, I've never been allowed to blend, in a natural and healthy manner, with the culture and civilization of the West." Again, Wright's immersion in a normative Chicago social science is detectable. What is "natural and healthy" has been, perforce, forestalled, but does this mean that this condition, the "pathology" of the Negro, is necessarily unnatural and unhealthy? "Me and my environment are one, but that oneness has in it, at its very heart, a schism. I regard my position as natural." Again, note the word "natural," which acquires a peculiar freight in Wright, where "nature" can be a threatening thing.

On the question of social identity, Wright seemed to relinquish the voluntarist model of elective affinity: "I have not consciously elected to be a Western: I have been made into a Western." (The process began, he said helpfully, in childhood.) And the content of his Westernness, he said, "resides fundamentally . . . in my secular outlook upon life." He was a humanist; he was a secularist; he believed that religion should be separate from the polity. "I feel that human personality is an end in and for itself. In short, I believe that man, for good or ill, is his own ruler, his own sovereign." Sovereign over all but his social identity. Human personality as an end in and for itself: yes, but personality abstracted from history. This is, of course, essentialist humanism, a doctrine, granted, that determines no politics in particular. (Compare, however, this passage from Burke's speech on the representation motion: "I know there is an order that keeps things fast in their place; it is made to us, and we are made to it. Why not ask another wife, other children, another body, another mind?") All quotes from Wright, "Tradition and Industrialization," 350.

38. Frantz Fanon, cited in Stuart Hall, "Cultural Identity and Cinematic Representation," *Framework* 36 (1989): 71.

39. See "Cornel West: With the People in Mind" (interview with bell hooks [Gloria Watkins]), *Emerge* 2, no. 1 (October 1990): 57.

40. Here the classic text would be Michael Oakeshott, "Rationalism in Politics," in *Rationalism in Politics and Other Essays* (New York: Basic Books, 1962), 1–36. What follows is a cento of Oakeshott describing his enemy, the rationalist: "To the Rationalist, nothing is of value merely because it exists (and certainly not because it has existed for many generations), familiarity has no worth, and nothing is to be left standing for want of scrutiny. . . . This assimilation of politics to engineering is, indeed, what may be called

the myth of rationalist politics. . . . If by chance this *tabula rasa* [the supposed blank sheet of infinite possibility] has been defaced by the irrational scribblings of tradition-ridden ancestors, then the first task of the Rationalist must be to scrub it clean. . . . What in the seventeenth century was L'art de penser has now become *Your mind and how to use it, a plan by world-famous experts for developing a trained mind at a fraction of the usual cost.* What was the Art of Living has become the *Technique of Success.* . . . Like Midas, the Rationalist is always in the unfortunate position of not being able to touch anything, without transforming it into an abstraction; he can never get a square meal of experience" (4–5).

41. Raymond Williams, *Culture and Society: 1780–1950* (London: Chatto and Windus, 1958).

Chapter Two: Fade to Black: From Cultural Studies to Cultural Politics

1. Kobena Mercer, "Travelling Theory: The Cultural Politics of Race and Representation: An interview with Kobena Mercer," *Afterimage* 18, no. 2 (September 1990): 8.

2. Patrick Brantlinger, *Crusoe's Footprints: Cultural Studies in Britain and America* (New York: Routledge, 1990), 38–40.

3. Raymond Williams, *Culture and Society* (London: Chatto and Windus, 1958), 4–5.

4. All these quotes from Williams are from ibid., 8–9, 11, and 12, respectively.

5. Stuart Hall cited in Francis Barker et al., eds., *Literature, Society, and the Sociology of Literature* (Colchester, UK: University of Essex, 1977).

6. The left hand, as I'm figuring it.

7. Which is the right hand of the Burkean equation.

8. What we know from Ben Anderson, the notion that "a nation is not an idea only of local extent, and individual momentary aggregation; but it is an idea of continuity, which extends in time as well as in numbers and in space" (Edmund Burke, *The Works of the Right Honorourable Edmund Burke* [London: Bohn's British Classics, 1854; hereafter referred to as *Works*], 6:147).

9. Raymond Williams, *Towards 2000* (London: Chatto and Windus, 1983), 193.

10. Quoted in Peter Hennessy, *The Prime Minister: The Office and Its Holders Since 1945* (London: Palgrave Macmillan, 2001), 205.

11. Paul Gilroy, *"There Ain't No Black in the Union Jack": The Cultural Politics of Race and Nation* (London: Hutchinson, 1987), 50.

12. Robert Young, "The Politics of 'The Politics of Literary Theory,'" *Oxford Literary Review* 10, nos. 1–2 (1988): 155.

13. Ibid.

14. Raymond Williams, *Culture and Society, 1780–1950* (New York: Columbia University Press, 1958).

15. Parry's own story focuses on the schism between cultural materialists and cultural discourse, between the perhaps incompatible perceptions "of radical humanist and postcolonial cosmopolitanism." But that's a tension that Hall has been forced to accommodate himself— containing, like Walt Whitman, multitudes—in order not to relinquish his ongoing relevance to both parties. Benita Parry, "The Contradictions of Cultural Studies," *Transition*, no. 53 (1991): 37–45.

16. Gilroy's contributions to *The Empire Strikes Back* (London: CCCS/Hutchinson, 1982) have significant affinities with what Michael Sandel has been doing with liberal communitarianism; they just have recourse to completely disjunct libraries.

17. Stuart Hall, "Minimal Selves," in *Identity—the Real Me (ICA Documents 6)*, ed. Homi K. Bhabha (London: Institute of Contemporary Arts, 1988), 44–46, 45. The politics of "infinite dispersal" would become, with the post-structuralist view of subjects, mere discursive smears and end by disassembling all fictions of human agency. We end up with monads, with atoms, not actors.

18. We shouldn't lose sight of the fact that Hall is, exemplarily, a public intellectual. And he played a significant role in revamping the British Communist Party in the early 1990s along these lines. The controversy occasioned by the manifesto of the revamped party, *New Times*, attests to the ability of such "post-Marxists" to disturb the *old* new left. And I would adduce a piece by the editor of *Race & Class*, A. Sivanandan, that displays that wonderful British gift for understatement: "New Times," he writes, "is a fraud, a counterfeit, a humbug. . . . New Times is Thatcherism in drag" (*Communities of Resistance: Writings on Black Struggles for Socialism* [London: Verso, 1990], 19). There's something revealing about Sivanandan's use of the metaphor of transvestitism to denigrate a politics that would be attuned to the positionalities associated with ethnicity, but also with sexual identity. It's the perturbing insertion of gritty and unsettling issues like gender in the smoothly oiled machine of *Race & Class* that people like Sivanandan find so infuriating.

19. Hall, "Minimal Selves," 44.

20. Isaac Kramnick, *The Rage of Edmund Burke: Portrait of an Ambivalent Conservative* (New York: Basic Books, 1977), 54.

21. "Partnership of past and present" is Burke's phrase.

22. Stuart Hall, "Cultural Identity and Cinematic Representation," *Framework* 36 (1989): 68–82.

23. As an acknowledgment of human agency—the political effectivity of human volition—voluntarism is frequently dismissed as a mystified fiction by those taken with deterministic social theories in which humans are mere cultural or structural dopes (to borrow Harold Garfinkle's derogation of Talcott Parsons). Anthony Appiah has written that an Althusserian account of "interpellation" can "put one in mind of *Invasion of the Body Snatchers*, pod-people and all" ("Tolerable Falsehoods: Agency and the Interests of Theory," in *Consequences of Theory*, ed. Barbara Johnson and Jonathan Arac [Baltimore, MD: Johns Hopkins University Press, 1991], 90).

24. Langston Hughes, *The Big Sea* (New York: Knopf, 1940), 228.

25. Imamu Amiri Baraka, *Home: Social Essays* (New York: Morrow, 1966), 216.

26. Richard Bruce Nugent, "Smoke, Lilies, and Jade," *Fire!!* (November 1926).

27. Mercer, "Travelling Theory."

28. Kobena Mercer and Isaac Julien, "De Margin and De Centre," introduction to "The Last Special Issue on Race," *Screen* 29, no. 4 (Autumn 1988): 1–12.

29. Manthia Diawara, ed., *Black American Cinema* (New York: Routledge, 1993), 206.

30. Manthia Diawara, "The Absent One: The Avant-Garde and the Black Imaginary in *Looking for Langston*," *Wide Angle* 13, nos. 3–4 (1991): 104.

31. Ibid., 108.

32. Coco Fusco, "Fantasies of Oppositionality," *Screen* 29, no. 4 (Autumn 1988), "Last Special Issue on Race," ed. Isaac Julien and Kobena Mercer; also reprinted in *Afterimage* 16, no. 5 (December 1988): 6.

33. Julien and Mercer, "De Margin and De Centre," 4.

34. Ernest Laclau and Chantal Mouffe, *Hegemony and Socialist Strategy: Towards a Radical Democratic Politics* (London: Verso, 1985), 121.

35. Edmund Burke, "SPEECH on a motion made in the House of Commons, the 7th of May 1782, for a Committee to Inquire into the state of the Representation of the Commons in Parliament," in Burke, *Works*, 6:145–146.

36. Paul Gilroy, "The Cruciality of the Frog's Perspective," *Third Text* (1989): 33–44; Kobena Mercer, "Black Art and the Burden of Representation," *Third Text* (1990): 41–78.

37. Paul Gilroy, *The Black Atlantic: Modernity and Double Consciousness* (Cambridge, MA: Harvard University Press, 1993).

38. Gilroy, "Cruciality and the Frog's Perspective," 282.

39. Kwame Anthony Appiah, "Social Forces, Natural Kinds," Science, Gender, and Race panel of the Radical Philosophers Association, American Philosophical Association Eastern Division Meeting, New York, December 1987. See also Kwame Anthony Appiah, *Cosmopolitanism: Ethics in a World of Strangers* (New York: Norton, 2006), for Appiah's fullest elaboration of this theory of identity; and Kwame Anthony Appiah, *The Ethics of Identity* (Princeton, NJ: Princeton University Press, 2005).

40. Frantz Fanon, *Black Skin, White Masks,* trans. Charles Lam Markmann (New York: Grove Press, 1967), 135.

41. Homi Bhabha, "Interrogating Identity: The Postcolonial Prerogative," in *The Anatomy of Racism,* ed. David Goldberg (Minneapolis: University of Minnesota Press, 1990), 183–209.

42. See my "Critical Remarks," in Goldberg, *The Anatomy of Racism.*

43. John Guillory, "Canon, Syllabus, List: A Note on the Pedagogic Imaginary," *Transition,* no. 52 (1991): 36–54.

44. Edward Said and Raymond Williams, "Media, Margins, and Modernity," in *The Politics of Modernism: Against the New Conformists,* ed. Tony Pinkney (London: Verso, 1989), 182.

45. Young, "The Politics."

46. I want to put my finger on a separate difficulty that runs through much political criticism and on equivocation that I take to be symptomatic. We tend to equivocate between, on the one hand, what a text *could* mean—the possibilities of its signification, the "modalities of the production of meaning," as de Man has it—and, on the other hand, what a text *does* mean, which is the issue of its actual political effectivity. Political criticism usually works by demonstrating the former and insinuating the latter. The political charge comes from the latter, the question of reception. But it's like, what are we, sociologists? Can't be bothered with much that now, can we? With a few exceptions, it's not what we lit crits were trained to do. But as political critics, we *trade* on that ambiguity (although saying so is considered rude). Mushnick's column appeared in *Sports Illustrated* on April 6, 1990; the cover story appeared on May 14, 1990.

47. Published as *Darker Than Blue* (Cambridge, MA: Harvard University Press, 2009).

48. I don't think this much of an extrapolation. In an issue of *Screen*, for instance, a distinguished avant-garde filmmaker, Yvonne Rainer, helpfully listed her conferential others: "Starting with the most victimized (alas, even the most noble fantasy of solidarity has its pecking order), they were: blacks, Lesbians, Latina women, Asians, and gay men." (She apologized that Latino men "got lost in the shuffle.") (Bérénice Reynaud and Yvonne Rainer, "Responses to Coco Fusco's 'Fantasies of Oppositionality,'" *Screen* 30 no. 3 [1989]: 91–92). Personally, I think they ought to be listed in alphabetical order, like on Oscar night.

49. Patricia J. Williams, *The Alchemy of Race and Rights* (Cambridge, MA: Harvard University Press, 1991).

Chapter Three: Critical Fanonism

1. *Frantz Fanon: Black Skin, White Masks*, directed by Isaac Julien, Arts Council of England, 1996; Robert J. C. Young, *Postcolonialism: An Historical Introduction* (Oxford, UK: Blackwell, 2001); David Macey, *Frantz Fanon: A Life* (London: Granta Books, 2000); Nigel Gibson, ed., *Rethinking Fanon: The Continuing Dialogue* (Amherst, NY: Humanity Books, 1999); Homi K. Bhabha, "Remembering Fanon: Self, Psyche, and the Colonial Condition," Foreword to *Black Skin, White Masks*, by Frantz Fanon (London: Pluto Press, 1986); Kwame Anthony Appiah, "Foreword," to *Black Skin, White Masks*, by Frantz Fanon (New York: Grove Press, 2008); Homi K. Bhabha, "Framing Fanon," in *The Wretched of the Earth*, by Frantz Fanon (New York: Grove Press, 2004), xv, xli.

2. Jerome McGann, "The Third World of Criticism," in *Rethinking Historicism: Critical Readings in Romantic History,* ed. Marjorie Levinson et al. (New York: Blackwell, 1989), 85–107; Donald Pease, "Toward a Sociology of Literary Knowledge: Greenblatt, Colonialism, and the New Historicism," in *Consequences of Theory: Selected Papers from the English Institute, 1987–1988,* ed. Barbara Johnson and Jonathan Arac (Baltimore, MD: Johns Hopkins University Press, 1991), 108–153.

3. A properly contextualized reading of the text to which I most frequently recur, *Black Skin, White Masks,* should situate it in respect to such germinal works as Jean-Paul Sartre, *Reflexions sur la Question Juive* (Paris: Morihien, 1946); O. Mannoni, *Psychologies de la Colonisation* (Paris, 1950); and Germaine Guex, *La Nevrose d'abandon* (Paris: Presses Universitaires de France, 1950), as well as many lesser-known works. But this is only to begin to sketch out the challenge of rehistoricizing Fanon.

4. Edward W. Said, "Representing the Colonized: Anthropology's Interlocutors," *Critical Inquiry* 15 (Winter 1989): 223.

5. Ibid., 223–225.

6. Albert Memmi, *The Colonized and the Colonizer,* trans. Howard Greenfeld (Boston: Beacon Press, 1967), 85.

7. Homi Bhabha, "Difference, Discrimination, and the Discourse of Colonialism," in *The Politics of Theory,* ed. Francis Barker et al., proceedings of the Essex Conference on the Sociology of Literature, July 1982 (Colchester, UK: University of Essex, 1983), 200.

8. Bhabha, "Remembering Fanon."

9. Homi K. Bhabha, "Signs Taken for Wonders: Questions of Ambivalence and Authority Under a Tree Outside Delhi,

May 1817," in *"Race," Writing, and Difference,* ed. Henry Louis Gates, Jr. (Chicago: University of Chicago Press, 1986), 169.

10. Bhabha, "Difference, Discrimination," 200.

11. Cited in Bhabha, "Remembering Fanon," xxv.

12. Benita Parry, "Problems in Current Theories of Colonial Discourse," *Oxford Literary Review* 9, nos. 1–2 (Winter 1987): 31.

13. Ibid., xiii.

14. Bhabha, "Remembering Fanon," xiv–xv.

15. Fanon, *Black Skin, White Masks,* 161n25.

16. Ibid., 162.

17. Bhabha, "Remembering Fanon," xviii.

18. Ibid., xix.

19. Ibid., xx.

20. Abdul R. JanMohamed, "The Economy of Manichean Allegory: The Function of Racial Difference in Colonial Literature," in *"Race," Writing, and Difference,* ed. Gates, 78, 79.

21. Stephen Heath, *"Le Pere Noel," October* 26 (Fall 1983): 77.

22. JanMohamed, "The Economy of Manichean Allegory," 83.

23. Ibid., 84.

24. Spivak may keep him company here. In "Three Women's Texts," she writes: "No perspective critical of imperialism can turn the Other into a self, because the project of imperialism has always already historically refracted what might have been the absolutely Other into a domesticated Other that consolidates the imperialist self" (in *"Race," Writing, and Difference,* ed. Gates, 272). The "absolutely Other" here seems to be something we find rather than make. I should stress that it's not the no-

tion of otherness as such but of absolute otherness that I want to question.

25. Parry, "Problems in Current Theories," 47.

26. Ibid., 29.

27. Ibid., 31–32.

28. Fanon, *Black Skin, White Masks*, 10.

29. Parry, "Problems in Current Theories," 43.

30. Ibid., 45.

31. Ibid., 43–44.

32. Gayatri Chakravorty Spivak, "Theory in the Margin, Coetzee's *Foe* Reading Defoe's *Crusoe/Roxana*," *English in Africa* 17, no. 2 (1990): 191–223.

33. Maria Loundoura, "Naming Gayatri Spivak" (interview with Spivak), *Stanford Humanities Review* 1, no. 1 (Spring 1989): 92.

34. Ibid., 92–93.

35. Ibid., 93.

36. Angela McRobbie, "Strategies of Vigilance: An interview with Gayatri Spivak," *Block* 10 (1985): 9.

37. Fanon, *Black Skin, White Masks*, 12.

38. See Stephen Greenblatt, *Renaissance Self-Fashioning* (Chicago: University of Chicago Press, 1980), 173, citing Sigmund Freud, *Civilization and Its Discontents*, trans. James Strachey (New York: Norton, 1962), 51.

39. Stephan Feuchtwang, "Fanonian Spaces," *New Formations* 1 (1993): 124–130, 127.

40. Fanon, *Black Skin, White Masks*, 13.

41. Albert Memmi, *The Colonized and the Colonizer* (Boston: Beacon Press, 1967), xiii.

42. Jean-Paul Sartre, "Preface" to *Wretched of the Earth*, by Frantz Fanon, trans. Constance Farrington (New York: Grove Press, 1968), 10.

43. McGann, "The Third World of Criticism," 86, 87.

44. Albert Memmi, review of *Fanon* by Peter Geismer and *Frantz Fanon* by David Caute, *New York Times Book Review*, March 14, 1971, 5. Bhabha, "Framing Fanon," xxxii. Bhabha cites Albert Memmi, "The Impossible Life of Frantz Fanon," *Massachusetts Review* (Winter 1973): 9–39; Albert Memmi, *Dominated Man: Notes Toward a Portrait* (New York: Orion Press, 1968); and Francois Vergès, *Monsters and Revolutionaries: Colonial Family Romances and Metissage* (Durham, NC: Duke University Press, 1999), 211.

45. Bhabha, "Framing Fanon," xxxii.

46. Ibid., xxxiii.

47. Memmi, review, 5; Bhabha, "Framing Fanon," xxxiii.

48. Memmi, review, 5.

49. Ibid.

50. Memmi, *Dominated Man*.

51. Ibid., 88.

52. Ibid.

53. Memmi, review, 5.

54. Fanon, *Black Skin, White Masks*, 15.

55. This chapter was originally prepared as a paper for and delivered (in abridged form) at the 1989 MSA panel on "Race and Psychoanalysis," at the invitation of Jane Gallop, which partly explains why my references to Fanon are largely to his first and most overtly psychoanalytic book, *Black Skin, White Masks*. Because Fanon's oeuvre receives scant attention in this chapter, I should remind readers unfamiliar with his works that early and late Fanon oppositional critics regard the later essays collected in, for example, *For the African Revolution* (New York: Monthly Review Press, 1967) to be his most valuable contribution.

Finally, I'm grateful to Benita Parry and Henry Finder, who commented on an earlier draft, even though I have failed to respond to their criticisms as I would have wished.

Chapter Four: Beyond the Culture Wars: Identities in Dialogue

1. Michael Tomasky, "Something New on the Mall," *New York Review of Books*, October 22, 2009, 4.

2. Adam Gopnik, "A Critic at Large: Read All About It," *New Yorker*, December 12, 1994, 12

3. "The Culture Warriors Get Laid Off," *New York Times*, March 14, 2009.

4. May 9 address at Liberty College, published in *Human Events*, May 23, 1992; cited in Garry Wills, "The Born-Again Republicans," *New York Review of Books*, September 24, 1992, 9.

5. In Will's review, "The foreign adversaries her husband Dick must keep at bay are less dangerous, in the long run, than the domestic forces with which she must deal. These forces are fighting against the conservation of the common culture that is the nation's social cement" (cited in Louis Menand, "What Are Universities For?" *Harper's* December 1991, 56).

6. Calvin Coolidge, "Are the 'Reds' Stalking Our College Women?" cited in Maurice Isserman, "Travels with Dinesh," *Tikkun*, September–October 1991, 81

7. John Guillory, *Cultural Capital: The Problem of Literary Canon Formation* (Chicago: University of Chicago Press, 1993), 13.

8. John Brenkman, "Multiculturalism and Criticism," in *English Inside and Out: The Places of Literary Criticism*, ed.

Susan Gubar and Jonathan Kamholtz (New York: Routledge, 1993), 98.

9. E. San Juan Jr., *Racial Formations/Critical Transformations: Articulations of Power in Ethnic and Racial Studies in the United States* (Atlantic Highlands, NJ: Humanities Press International, 1992), 132.

10. Hazel Carby, "Multi-culture," *Screen* 34 (Spring 1980): 64–65.

11. Guillory, *Cultural Capital*, 47.

12. Brenkman, "Multiculturalism and Criticism," 97.

13. Jean-Loup Amselle, *Affirmative Exclusion: Cultural Pluralism and the Rule of Custom in France,* trans. Jane Marie Todd (Ithaca, NY: Cornell University Press, 2003).

14. Guillory, *Cultural Capital,* 13.

15. Working Papers of the John F. Kennedy Institute, Freie Universität, Berlin, No. 55, Higham, John: Multiculturalism in Disarray, Johns Hopkins University, Department of History, Baltimore, MD, 1992 (History).

16. Brenkman, "Multiculturalism and Criticism," 89.

17. J. G. A. Pocock, *Politics, Language, and Time* (New York: Athenaeum, 1971), 85.

18. Brenkman, "Multiculturalism and Criticism," 95.

19. Ibid., 99.

20. Richard Rorty, "Pragmatism, Relativism, Irrationalism," in *Consequences of Pragmatism,* by Richard Rorty (Minneapolis: University of Minnesota Press, 1982), 166.

21. Peter Winch, *The Idea of a Social Science and Its Relation to Philosophy* (London: Routledge and Kegan Paul, 1958), 15.

22. F. Allan Hanson, *Meaning in Culture* (London: Routledge, 1975); Roy Wagner, *The Invention of Culture* (Englewood Cliffs, NJ: Prentice-Hall, 1975). See John M.

Beattie, "Objectivity and Social Anthropology," in *Objectivity and Cultural Divergence*, ed. S. C. Brown (Cambridge: Cambridge University Press, 1984), 1–20.

23. Kwasi Wiredu, *Philosophy and an African Culture* (Cambridge: Cambridge University Press, 1980), 220–221.

24. Martin Hollis, "Reason and Ritual," *Philosophy* 43 (1967): 240.

25. Isaiah Berlin, "Alleged Relativism in Eighteenth-Century European Thought," in Isaiah Berlin, *The Crooked Timber of Humanity: Chapters in the History of Ideas,* by Isaiah Berlin, ed. Henry Hardy (New York: Knopf, 1991), 85.

26. Isaiah Berlin, "The Pursuit of the Ideal," in *The Crooked Timber of Humanity*, 11.

27. Ibid., 12–13.

28. Ibid., 19.

29. John Higham, *Hanging Together: Unity and Diversity in American Culture*, ed. Carl J. Guarneri (New Haven, CT: Yale University Press, 2001), 234.

30. Alasdair MacIntyre, *Three Rival Versions of Moral Enquiry: Encyclopedia, Genealogy, and Tradition* (South Bend, IN: University of Notre Dame Press, 1990), 231.

31. Charles M. Blow, "An Article of Faith," *New York Times*, April 3, 2010, p. A17.

Index